FLY
WITHOUT FEAR

FLY
WITHOUT FEAR

Carol Stauffer
Captain Frank Petee

Dodd, Mead & Company • New York

No part of this book may be reproduced in any form
without permission in writing from the publisher.
Published by Dodd, Mead & Company, Inc.
71 Fifth Avenue, New York, New York 10003
Manufactured in the United States of America
First Edition

1   2   3   4   5   6   7   8   9   10

Library of Congress Cataloging-in-Publication Data

Stauffer, Carol.
    Fly without fear.

    Includes index.
    1. Fear of flying.   I. Petee, Frank.   II. Title.
RC1090.S73   1988   616.85′225   88-7087
ISBN 0-396-09293-4 (pbk.)

Book design and production by Eric Newman

Contents

Acknowledgments

This book could not have been written if it were not for the USAir Fearful Flyers Program, and we wish to thank the many people who believed in the program and helped us with it.

We are grateful to Edwin I. Colodny, USAir's chairman and president, for recognizing the need for such a program and for his continued support of it. Thanks to Nancy Vaughan, manager of public relations, for her ongoing encouragement and expert assistance in launching each class.

A special thanks to all the wonderful people who were there with us in the beginning: Jackie Hyman, who helped develop the program and co-direct it for several years; Dave Shipley; Julie Rothery; and Captains Bill Leefe and Larry Trapp. And a special appreciation to Jack O'Neill, who spent many hours "on the road" with us, giving of his expertise.

The continued success of the program is due to those who came along later: Captain Skip Budny, whose lectures and slide presentations have reassured many fearful flyers; Marty Lees; Pete Opar; Jim Frazier; and Joe D'Arcangelo.

We wish that we could list the names of all the pilots and flight attendants who have given so freely of their time and talent to help the fearful flyers.

As we travel to different cities and airports each year, we get expert assistance from the USAir sales, system control, customer service and maintenance staffs, the air-traffic controllers, and Sam Cooper. Thanks!

Sandra Joseph Galton is responsible for all the typing and much more, and we thank her for her expertise and patience. We are also indebted to Pat Hass and Barbara Beckman, our editors at Dodd, Mead & Company.

We *especially* want to recognize and thank our families for their patience and understanding, and we hope that they still recognize us!

And finally, our gratitude to all our former fearful flyers. We've admired your courage, loved knowing you, and thank you for helping us to write this book.

FLY
WITHOUT FEAR

Introduction

Fly without Fear was written in response to the many phone calls and letters that we receive every day from fearful flyers. We are the co-directors of the highly successful USAir Fearful Flyers Program, and people contact us to inquire about the program and how to enroll. These people are desperately seeking help to overcome their fear of flying.

The USAir Fearful Flyers program was developed in 1975 and is currently offered in ten cities each year. More than 2,000 fearful flyers have taken the course, and 97 *percent* of them are now able to fly relaxed and in comfort as a result of the program! Some of these people had never flown, some had not flown for years, and many were able to fly but hated every minute of it. The program worked for them all.

During our years of working with fearful flyers, we have learned much about how the fear develops, what people are afraid of, *and* how to overcome that fear. We have found that the most successful program combines behavior modification methods (relaxation training, "thought stopping" therapy, and desensitization) *and* aviation education (pilot training, operation and maintenance of airplanes, weather conditions, and, especially, turbulence).

Unfortunately, we cannot reach all of the fearful flyers who could benefit from the course. We wish that other airlines would start similar programs to help fill the vast need. Many people are disappointed when they discover that no program is offered in their area, and they frequently ask if there is a book or other materials that they could read.

We realized that there was a need for such a book— one written by authors who have experience and expertise working with fearful flyers. We felt that we had all the necessary credentials to do this. One author is a therapist trained and experienced in behavior modification methods, and the other is an airline professional with many years' flying experience as well as training and managerial exper- tise—authors who have years of experience working with large numbers of fearful flyers and evidence that their methods are successful in overcoming the fear of flying.

We wish that every one of you could take the USAir Fearful Flyers Program, as we feel that it is the best way to overcome the fear of flying. *And* we would like to meet each and every one of you. Since that isn't possible, we have put all of the aviation education (even some extras!) and step- by-step instructions on how to use the behavior modifica- tion methods from our class into this book. In addition, there are interesting case studies, information on fears and phobias, and much, much more. It is *the same information and methods* that have helped thousands of fearful flyers to overcome their fear of flying.

Now it can help you!

CHAPTER 1

Who Are the Fearful Flyers?

"When they closed that door and I knew I couldn't get off, I felt trapped."

"My hands were cold and clammy, my heart began to pound, and I felt overwhelmed by fear."

"I was afraid of panicking and losing control."

"I just wanted to jump out of my seat and start running—I had to get off!"

Esther, fifty-four, has a successful law practice in Washington, D.C. She is outgoing, articulate, and bold—not the sort of person you would suspect of being afraid of flying. But every time she flies, she updates her will and then sits and writes letters to her three sons, telling them that she "didn't want to die this way." She hates turning her life over to someone else—someone she has never met and knows nothing about. She compensates for this lack of control by spending the entire flight feeling that she has to "hold the plane up." She has to stay in her seat, hold on to the arms, and "help" the pilot fly the plane. If she relaxes for a moment, she is certain, something terrible will happen. She especially dreads the mandatory pre-flight emergency instructions, which describe how to use the seat as a life preserver.

Barry, thirty-eight, lives in Pittsburgh and is employed as a sales representative by a large corporation. He wears conservative business suits and carries a briefcase, but he has one trait that doesn't seem to fit his corporate image: He is deathly afraid of flying. Barry has been known to take twenty-four-hour train rides from Pittsburgh to Atlanta— via Washington—to avoid a two-hour flight. His boss seems understanding, but Barry believes that his fear has held back his career. When he flew in the past, he became anxious weeks before his flight. Once aboard, he strapped himself into his seat—never a window seat—and refused to get up. "I felt lightheaded . . . dizzy . . . I was as white as a ghost. I felt certain the plane was going down. When we landed, I wanted to kiss the ground and vowed that I would never fly again."

Helen, also thirty-eight, a teacher in Albany, New York, has suffered from aviaphobia since she was eighteen. Twenty years later, she is old enough to know better. And smart enough, too. She is the president of a national women's organization and a biology teacher, and she knows that it's no big deal to get on a plane and fly somewhere. After all, people do it every day. "I'm afraid of heights; I'm afraid of elevators; I'm afraid of mountains—I have all kinds of phobias. I know claustrophobia is a part of it. I hate being stuck in the air for three or four hours and not being able to get out. I get queasy when I make the reservations. And once I'm on the plane, I don't even need a seat—I just head for the bathroom." Personal and professional demands require that Helen fly, and so she does. But each journey means hours of pre-flight anxiety, an airborne bout of nausea and diarrhea, and the desperate realization that she will have to get on another plane to return home.

These three people want to fly. They feel ashamed and embarrassed that they can't get on a plane and fly like "normal" people. They have tried alcohol, drugs, and psychotherapy without success.

Fearful flyers are not just little old ladies who have never flown or people who gave up flying because they were in an accident or knew someone who was. In reality, most fearful flyers are able to drag themselves onto an airplane, and many are even frequent flyers.

In 1980, a Boeing Aircraft study estimated that 25 million Americans, or one out of every six adults, are afraid to fly.[1] And these were only the ones who admitted their fear. Fearful flyers are of all ages, they are men and women, and they may be the people sitting around you on the plane. That fearful flyer may even be you!

SPOTTING OTHER FEARFUL FLYERS

You probably think that you're the only one on the plane who is fearful. Everyone else seems to be in good spirits, and some people are actually eating, reading, or even sleeping!

But look around. How about that gentleman calling to the flight attendant? "How soon will you be serving drinks?" he asks. He may be an anxious flyer who hopes that a drink will bolster his courage. Or what about that woman taking some pills from her purse? Are they aspirin for a headache or tranquilizers to help her make it through the flight?

A man in Orlando changed airlines because the first one ran out of gin before he reached his destination. A Rochester woman couldn't tell you how many miles it was from Rochester to other cities—but she knew how many drinks it was. Mary lived in Detroit and had to attend monthly business meetings in New York City. She had to take a few drinks, and/or tranquilizers just to get on the plane. Once, she took so many that she made it to the meeting but fell asleep in the middle of it. Others might not fall asleep but are so exhausted by the time they arrive that they need a day or two to recuperate. Then, as soon as they start to feel rested and relaxed, they have to worry about getting on the plane to return home. *Anxiety and tension take a heavy toll on the human body.*

A fearful flyer may also be the passenger who is unable to get out of his seat for any reason. These people may never see the inside of a rest room on a plane—even on long flights.

Some fearful flyers are afraid of upsetting the balance of the plane or wonder if the floor is sturdy enough to hold a number of people walking around at the same time. And still others grip the arms of their seats and go through every maneuver right along with the pilot.

Fearful flyers are overly sensitive to noises or a lack of noises on an aircraft—sounds they might ignore on a bus or a train. They tense visibly or jump when the landing gear is retracted or the engines become quiet. When one woman looked out of the plane's window and saw the wing flaps being lowered, she called to the flight attendant, "Does the captain know this wing is broken?"

Frightened people are also extremely concerned about turbulence, and a turbulent flight can cause an anxious person to give up flying altogether. In fact, these people are convinced that the plane is in danger of falling apart or suffering some structural damage, and they think that the plane drops or rises thousands of feet during turbulence. No wonder they're afraid!

PHYSICAL SIGNS OF ANXIETY

The symptoms of anxiety can range in intensity from a vague uneasiness and apprehension to a feeling of terror and panic. These feelings can cause the body to react in various uncomfortable and frightening ways. Which of the following do you experience when flying or thinking about flying?

- Trembling or shaking
- Weakness in legs
- Cold hands or feet
- Sweating
- Chest heaviness or tightness
- Muscle tension
- Heart palpitations
- Urinary frequency
- Diarrhea
- Shortness of breath or even hyperventilation
- Nausea or vomiting
- Feelings of choking or suffocating

These symptoms may occur weeks in advance of the actual flight. Just thinking about flying can set them off. As the time of the flight approaches, the feelings become more intense. Many people can't sleep; some have nightmares. These feelings can become so uncomfortable and frightening that people will do anything to avoid them. They then stop flying altogether or fly only when it's unavoidable.

When someone falls off a horse, the common response is to tell him or her to get right back on in order to overcome the fear of falling again. Family and friends may say to fearful flyers, "Come on, get on the plane; you'll be fine." But it doesn't usually work that way. *Continuing to fly after you've developed a fear may make it worse, not better.* For example:

- You begin to have physical symptoms.
- Now you have to worry about flying *and* the physical symptoms.
- Every time you fly, you experience these symptoms.
- It becomes more and more difficult to put yourself in a situation that induces these symptoms.
- These symptoms and feelings become more and more connected to an airplane as you continue to fly.

WHY SO FEARFUL?

Most fearful flyers have never been in an airline accident nor had a bad experience while flying. So why are they so afraid? The fear of flying is often the result of another phobia or a combination of phobias. Fearful flyers may be afraid of closed spaces, heights, crashing and/or dying, or not being in control. We gave the following survey to one hundred fearful flyers to discover what, exactly, they feared.

We asked, "Which of the following are responsible for your fear?"

- Acrophobia (fear of heights)
- Claustrophobia (fear of closed places)
- Fear of crashing/dying
- A previous bad flying experience
- Not being in control of the situation
- Other

SURVEY RESULTS

Fear or phobia	Percent reporting this as a cause of their problem[a]
Acrophobia	39
Claustrophobia	44
Fear of crashing/dying	30
A previous bad flying experience	29
Not being in control of the situation	77
Other	1[b]

[a] Most people have more than one fear/phobia that makes flying traumatic.
[b] Fear of going too fast, among others.

Note that seventy-seven out of one hundred people feared not being in control of the situation. Fearful flyers are often achieving, successful people who are used to being in control of their lives. They hold prestigious positions, are well educated, and function very well in society. They like to feel that they have some control over events in their lives. We always ask our class members how many would rather drive the car than be a passenger in it. Invariably, almost all of them (and the instructors, too) raise their hands.

However, not all fearful flyers do feel in control of their lives. Many suffer from other fears and phobias in addition to the fear of flying. Some are agoraphobics—fearful of separation from familiar surroundings or people. They have often overcome many fears already, and the fear of flying is a final challenge.

THE FOUR FLYING FEARS

Acrophobia, claustrophobia, fear of crashing/dying, and fear of not being in control are the four major flying fears.

"A previous bad flying experience" falls into a separate category. Often, a lack of information is to blame. People think that something serious happened to put them in extreme danger, when in fact it did not. It's true that once in a great while a problem may occur during a flight. But most of the time the things that traumatize people are ordinary events that present no danger whatsoever. We discuss this issue later in the book; for now, let's look at the four main fears connected with flying.

Acrophobia (fear of heights)

It is thought that babies have only two fears at birth: the fear of loud noises and the fear of falling. It seems natural, then, that some people will develop a fear of heights and that some of these people will develop a fear of flying. Passengers with a fear of heights stay away from window seats and hate it when the captain announces, "We are now flying at an altitude of 30,000 feet." They often wish the plane would fly just a few hundred feet above the ground for the entire flight, even though they know that they would be in as much danger if they fell 200 feet as they would be if they fell 2,000 feet. Acrophobics may also fear going into tall buildings, crossing bridges, or riding on escalators and amusement-park rides.

Surprisingly, some acrophobics do *not* have a fear of flying. When they are in an airplane, they feel completely enclosed, so for them it is not the same as standing in a high place or being on an amusement-park ride.

Claustrophobia (fear of closed spaces)

It's also understandable why people who fear being closed in may also fear airplanes. First of all, in most airport terminals, one must walk down a long, narrow jetway with no windows to get onto an airplane. Once inside the plane, one looks down a long, narrow aisle with seats set closely together on either side. Sitting down, passengers discover that the seat is not very wide and that generally there is another person sitting quite close on one or both sides. Short people may not be able to see over the seat in front, tall people may find insufficient space to put their legs. Next, one must fasten a seat belt and keep it fastened until someone says that you can unfasten it.

Then, lots of people come crowding down the aisle, cramming things into overhead compartments and stuffing more under the seats. Will they *ever* all get seated? And who gets to use the arm rest, you or your seatmate? What if he's a six-foot-plus basketball player who sprawls over into your small space? Finally, everyone is seated, and you try to relax. But wait—they're closing the door and aren't going to open it until you reach your destination! And the windows don't open either.

Several years ago, a woman called us and said that her family was going to disown her. They were tired of driving seemingly endless miles to take a vacation and said that either she had to fly next year or they were going on vacation without her. She had claustrophobia and could not get on an airplane. She said, "I could fly anywhere in the world if they would just leave that outside door open."

Once you reach your destination, it's even worse. Everyone is in a hurry and crowds into the aisle as soon as the plane arrives at the gate. They begin pulling their belongings out of the compartments and stand in the aisles, packed like sardines, waiting for the door to open (maybe some of them are claustrophobics too).

Claustrophobics may also fear going into elevators, tunnels, caves, and small rest rooms.

Fear of crashing/dying

People who fear crashing or dying worry that they are in real danger every time they fly. In most cases, this is due to a lack of knowledge. On a turbulent flight, they think that the plane will break up or that the pilots can't control it. They worry that the pilot didn't get enough sleep the night before or may be drinking or taking drugs. Their fear of dying is transmitted to the airplane, and this causes them to become very anxious each time they fly or stop flying altogether. These people may develop their fear after having children; they also may not like being far from home. Before each flight, they write wills, clean their houses, listen to every weather report, and take out insurance policies.

Fear of not being in control

Passengers on an aircraft have to give up control to someone else. They have to stay in their seats with their seat belts fastened and turn their lives over to someone else—a person they may never see. They can't question the pilot's qualifications, help the pilot fly the plane, or ask to be let off when they feel they've had enough. In addition, most of us don't know how the plane stays up, how qualified the mechanics are, or if the air-traffic controllers are stable and trustworthy people.

People who like to be in control worry about all aspects of the flight. One man told us he worries most about the takeoff. "Is the runway long enough? Is the plane going too fast or too slow? Does it have enough power to make it off the ground? I feel I have to stay very alert, hold my breath, and *will* the plane up."

Another fearful flyer says, "I don't worry about the plane getting up. I wonder how it's going to *stay* up there. When the engines all of a sudden get quiet, I *know* the plane is going to fall right out of the sky! I spend the entire flight 'helping' the pilot keep the plane up there and listening for any unusual sounds."

"Well, I hate the landing," mutters a third flyer. "I'm sure the plane isn't going to stop in time and that there isn't enough runway anyway. I brace my feet on the floor, hold very still, and 'help' the pilot bring the plane to a stop."

These people are unable to sit back, relax, and give up control to someone else. They may also be people who would rather drive a car than be a passenger, don't like to be hypnotized or relaxed, and want to be informed about everything that is happening in a given situation. Virginia and David were two such people.

Virginia, twenty-nine, lives in Cleveland, Ohio. She is so afraid to fly, so worried about leaving the solid earth, that she ducks underneath the dashboard of the family car and buries her face in the seat on the way to the airport to catch a flight. Her phobia is so strong that she becomes panicky at the sight of airplanes at the airport. Her fear of flying means that she and her husband, Marty, must drive to vacation spots such as Cape Cod—fifteen hours from Cleveland—

instead of beginning their holiday by boarding a plane. Marty tolerated the inconvenience created by Virginia's phobia until his employer awarded him a two-week, all-expenses-paid vacation to Hawaii. Virginia and Marty never took that vacation because of her fear of flying, and Marty announced that she had to conquer her fear.

David is a forty-three-year-old businessman who owns his own travel agency. He has missed out on trips to Japan, Italy, and other exotic places because he can't get on an airplane. What do his employees think about his fear? "They know I travel a lot," he says. "I just don't tell them I'm going by train. I fly my family to Florida and tell the kids that Daddy is driving because he has business stops to make along the way. I developed the fear after having children. I'm afraid of crashing and leaving my children without a father. The first time I flew to Florida we went through a thunderstorm. I don't like turbulence, and I was scared the entire flight. Every time the plane 'dropped,' I knew it was all over."

CONQUERING YOUR FEAR

Maybe you can identify with Virginia and David or the three fearful flyers discussed in the beginning of this chapter. They are all now fearless flyers, able to fly anywhere in the world, comfortably and relaxed. They overcame their fears using the methods discussed in this book. These methods include behavior modification techniques and aviation education.

Progressive relaxation exercises, a cognitive therapy— "thought stopping"—and desensitization methods will enable you to relax your body and mind and fly comfortably.

> **A Thought to Fly by**
>
> You can't be tense and relaxed at the same time.

The aviation education will inform you about pilot training, flight operations, and design and maintenance of planes. We will also cover weather conditions and turbulence and explain how the air-traffic control system operates.

> **A Thought to Fly by**
>
> The more you understand about something, the less fearsome it will be.

These methods will enable you to control your fear instead of letting it control you and your life. It doesn't matter if you have never flown, haven't flown for years, or fly but hate every minute of it. It doesn't matter how you acquired the fear or how long you have had it. We can help you overcome it!

Read on. Enjoy the book. Enjoy the flying!

CHAPTER 2

Clearing Away the Mists and the Myths of Flying

MISCONCEPTIONS AND CLOSE CALLS

Conversations with fearful flyers are often based on *misses*. They talk about near-*miss*es, *miss*ing engines, and *miss*ed approaches. Their fears generally stem from *mis*conceptions about airplanes.

One basic misconception about flying is that an airplane in flight is simply suspended in empty space—almost as if only a thin thread were holding it up. And it would take almost nothing—perhaps a failed engine or a lightning strike—to cut the thread. Then the airplane would fall straight down out of the sky.

Even a simple misunderstanding can keep someone out of airplanes for a long time, if not forever. Take Sandy: She had avoided flying for years, except for the occasional, absolutely necessary business trips. On one of these trips, while the plane was taxiing out for takeoff, the captain announced, "Folks, there are some thunderstorms in the area; you've probably seen occasional lightning flashes outside. After takeoff, we'll be making some turns to stay well clear of any turbulence connected with them. We should be away from them shortly after departure."

"But," Sandy said, "we weren't! The lightning was flashing all around us for the whole four-hour trip. It was terrible. I didn't eat. I couldn't go back to the bathroom. I decided once more as we were landing that I would never fly again."

Then, somewhat sheepishly, she confessed, "On the way out of the plane, I complained to a flight attendant that with all that lightning flashing around, we could have been struck. The attendant was nonplussed at first, then explained to me that there hadn't been any lightning after we took off; I must have been seeing the airplane's navigation lights flashing outside, reflecting against the clouds. If I hadn't said something to her, that misunderstanding might have stopped my flying forever."

Another example concerns a doctor who flew all the time because he had to. Recently in a class, he told us, "Of course I've had many close calls."

Not a person there questioned him or thought his statement strange. But I asked him, "Doctor, I assume by 'close calls' you mean you were in life-threatening situations?"

"Well, sure," he answered, sounding a trifle puzzled.

"I've been flying for more than fifty years," I said then. "I have almost 23,000 hours in the air, and I've never had a 'close call.' I've never been in what I consider a life-threatening situation."

In fact, even though many people share the doctor's misconception about flying in airplanes, I know thousands of pilots, and I know very few who have had what the doctors terms "close calls." Fearful people think that any time, every time, they're on a plane trip, they're close to knocking at death's door. Or if the plane gets through the flight without serious incident, they feel extremely lucky and thank their deities.

But the close calls and the bad experiences that fearful flyers talk about and often use as reasons never to fly again would not in most cases have the same connotations for nonfearful flyers. A rejected or aborted takeoff or landing, an announcement that a plane has a mechanical problem, a bout with turbulence—none of these constitutes a life-threatening situation. They're delaying but not dangerous.

A Thought to Fly by

Ninety-nine and ninety-nine one-hundredths per-cent of all airline flights are routine and normal.

FLYING SAFE—EXCEPT IN THE MEDIA

It's not surprising that fearful people "create" their own life-threatening situations. Isn't that what they, and you, have learned from the news and entertainment media? Most of the time, when there's an airplane story on television, in a movie, on the radio, or in the newspaper, the airplane has crashed or blown up or is lost, or, at the very least, the pilots were fighting in the cockpit. Because the media do not cover the safe, uneventful flights, many people learn to fear flying. The media present the spectacular and negative aspects of aviation. Statistics can seem distorted, and even minor incidents and accidents can be exaggerated. Possibly the most damage results from repetition, embellishing, and rehashing of coverage. The 1982 Air Florida accident in Washington, D.C., was featured on the front of the *Washington Post*, frequently with photographs, for *nine* days. Little wonder that fearful flyers think that air travel is not safe. But it is the safest form of travel. It's far safer than travel in your automobile or on your bicycle. You're safer stepping into an airliner than into your bathroom.

MISCONCEPTIONS AND TAKEOFFS

Many people worry about airplanes' getting off the ground. They agitate through each takeoff. "How can this huge, metal monster leave the ground and fly?" they think. Even those who do accept the planes' lifting off think that the planes have to use up most of the runway before they do so. Actually, when airliners take off they use only one-half to two-thirds of the available runway.

It's just as easy for a giant 747 with its big, powerful engines to take off with 400 people aboard as it is for a small trainer airplane to take off and fly with two people in it. The only differences are the power of the engines and the size of the wings and tail—the "airfoils." There's no magic involved.

Many people think that when an airplane is taking off, its engines are straining at full power—that they're working as hard as they can to get the huge, heavy hulk off the ground. Right? Wrong. Engines set at takeoff power are seldom using their full power. There's still a reserve available; if the pilot wants even more power, he or she can push the power levers farther forward and get more. (This is similar to a driver's "flooring" a car's accelerator.) Also, the pilots may even have computed a lower-than-maximum takeoff power if the load aboard is lighter than the maximum allowed for the airplane type.

ENGINE SOUNDS AND SILENCES

Some people worry about the various noises they hear while on an airplane. During takeoff, the engines make a lot of noise; the amount of noise heard varies with where one is sitting in relation to the engines. They're roaring as the plane rushes down the runway. Then the plane lifts off, it points upward, and perhaps the noise stops. It might quiet down suddenly and the plane seems to stop, too, and you know that in another minute it's going to fall. You *know* the engines have stopped and that the huge mass of metal is going to fall out of the sky. But it won't!

Why the sudden silence? If this occurs during a takeoff it's because of an air-traffic control restriction. The flight may have been instructed to level off at an intermediate altitude—4,000 feet is a good example—instead of climbing directly to its assigned cruising altitude.

Engine sound decreased because the pilot pulled the power, or thrust, levers back to decrease engine power to keep the plane within regulation air speeds. All aircraft flying below 10,000 feet in the United States are restricted to flying no faster than 250 knots airspeed (288 miles per hour). This is to slow the faster airplanes down to keep the speeds of all aircraft closer together, making air-traffic controllers' jobs somewhat easier. When the flight is cleared to resume its climb, the pilot increases power, and the sound returns.

CAN WE FLY WITHOUT ENGINES?

So the engines didn't quit, and the airplane didn't fall out of the sky. But what if an engine *did* fail? The plane would continue to fly! If one engine is shut down on a two-engine plane, it will continue to fly as long as there is fuel for the remaining engine. Actually, air regulations and policies require that, with one engine out on a twin-engine plane, a landing be made at the nearest suitable airport. That doesn't mean the nearest suitable cow pasture. It means a suitable airport.

If we were flying a three-engine airplane and shut an engine down, the plane would continue to fly on the remaining engines. If we then shut down another engine, it would still continue to fly on the remaining engine. Let's fly a four-engine airplane. If we shut down three of the four, the craft would continue to fly on one engine. We won't tell you that a huge 747 will continue to carry its heavy load at 40,000 feet on one powerplant. But if a descent is made to a lower, denser air altitude, it will continue to fly on one engine. The airplane will not fall out of the sky just because an engine fails or is stopped by its flight crew.

ENGINE DEPENDABILITY

Consider how dependable our powerplants actually are. Even the piston engines driving the propellers of planes a few years back were quite dependable, much more so than the public thought. Even so, an airline pilot could count on a few failures during the years he flew commercially. But with the jet engines, the turbine engines in use today, a young pilot starting out with the airlines will very likely go through his or her entire flying career without "losing" an engine—or even shutting it down as a precautionary measure to save it.

Pilots shut down an engine when there are symptoms of impending problems for a number of reasons: (1) They don't *need* to use it; (2) they're saving an expensive powerplant (worth millions of dollars each) from serious damage; and (3) they're saving it in case they have a greater need for it later in the flight—a good operating policy.

FLIGHT WITH *NO* POWER

What if, for some reason, a plane found itself up in the air with no power? Would it just fall out of the sky? No—it would glide. And planes can glide a long distance. This distance varies with the type of aircraft, its weight, and other factors. An example: If an airplane started gliding from one mile high, it could glide to a landing within fifteen miles in any direction. If it were two miles high, it could glide thirty miles, and so on.

Sometimes people ask, "Can the plane really land without any engine running?" The answer is yes. Think about gliders and sailplanes. They don't even have engines; they must be towed aloft by a powered plane and then cut free. They then glide back to earth. Sailplanes can delay the earthly return by finding and using thermals: updrafts, vertical air currents that can help the craft climb ever higher and soar great distances. (Heavy airliners are not capable of soaring in this manner, but they do glide.)

Each one of you has seen, at least on television, an aircraft about the size and weight of a DC–9 airliner landing without engines—the space shuttle. It doesn't even have engines, at least no engines that operate in our atmosphere. From the time it leaves its orbit in space, it is gliding to a landing, just like a DC–9, a Cessna two-seater, or the supersonic Concorde. They all glide. Pilots begin learning to glide their training planes to a safe landing without power before their first solo flight.

We once got a skeptical question: "Are you certain that the plane will glide the way you described it? Have you tried it?"

"We 'try' it almost every time we fly," we assured our questioner. "Let's say we're up at a high altitude and Airway Traffic Control clears us to descend to a much lower level. The pilot would pull his power levers all the way back, closed. This is the same as your taking your foot off your gas pedal; your auto's engine and the plane's engines are idling. In planes, we call this 'flight idle.' The amount of thrust moving us forward is not very different from that when the engines have been completely cut off. The pilot lowers the aircraft's nose a few degrees; the airplane now glides to the lower altitude."

A MISCONCEPTION AND THE IMPORTANT OCEAN OF AIR

Look closer at a popular misconception mentioned earlier in this chapter—that of the plane flying in empty space, seemingly held up by a thin thread. If the thread is broken, the plane falls out of the sky, straight down. ("Like a stone," one woman said.)

Actually, the plane is supported in very solid air. It's being held up by its wings and tail surfaces (its "airfoils"), supported just as a ship is on the ocean. It's supported by an ocean of air. This is the way you should think about it from now on.

This ocean of air is quite solid. You may not realize it because you can wave your hands around in it quite easily. But the faster you're moving through the air, the more solid it is. And you know that, if you think about it. Remember the first time you stuck your hand or arm out the window of a moving car? You were probably surprised to find that the air had force, even pressure; it pushed your hand back. If the car speeded up, even more force drove your hand or arm back, maybe even enough to bang it against the window frame. Air is actually fluid, and it can, in effect, be compressed. The faster your hand—or an airplane—moves through air, the more force the air has. If you compare the force against your hand at thirty-five miles per hour with the force at fifty-five miles per hour, think how solid the air would feel if you could put your hand outside an airplane traveling at hundreds of miles an hour!

A Thought to Fly by

The flying airplane is held up by an ocean of air.

A FIRST LOOK AT
THE FOUR FORCES OF FLIGHT

Four forces—thrust, lift, drag, and gravity—act on the airplane in the air. On a typical flight, the first force we feel is the *thrust*, or power, of the engines, pushing or pulling us forward. As we move faster, *lift* is created by the wing's curved shape. When there's enough lift, the airplane can rise off the ground, and we fly. When the plane is moving forward through the air, it encounters a force opposite to thrust called *drag*. We streamline automobiles and airplanes to reduce the frontal surface moving through the air, and this reduces dragging through the air.

When you first stuck your hand out the window of a moving car, it was the drag created by your hand that moved it backward. When you pushed forward, harder against the air's force—increasing the thrust—your hand moved forward again.

In flight, the thrust has to overcome the drag to move the plane forward. Lift is exceeding *gravity*, or the plane's weight, when it lifts off and climbs skyward. Look at Figure 2.1. This airplane is in level flight. The force arrows point in the direction(s) force is exerted.

The arrows denoting lift and gravity (weight) are equal in length. This is because the forces are balanced; the airplane is neither ascending nor descending. The thrust arrow is longer than the drag arrow. The plane is moving forward; thrust is stronger than drag.

Figure 2.1. Forces in level flight.

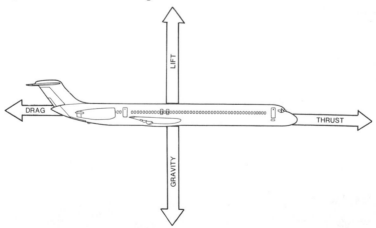

So what occurs when we lose (or don't use) our power, our thrust? How can we maintain the swift airflow we need over the wings to create lift? We substitute gravity for thrust. The pilot lowers the aircraft's nose slightly. Gravity imparts forward force, the same as engine thrust did. If we look at our force arrows from the airplane side view (Figure 2.2), now, instead of an arrow straight forward and one straight down, we instead see one at an angle, in between "forward" and "down." The airplane is gliding. In effect, airplanes glide to every landing, although a combination of engine thrust and gravity is normally used.

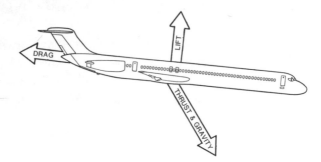

Figure 2.2. Gliding flight forces.

A Thought to Fly by

A plane without power wouldn't fall. It would glide.

WINGS, OR AIRFOILS, CREATE LIFT

We just demonstrated that a plane's lift can be generated either by using engine thrust or gravity. The lift is developed on the aircraft's curved wing and tail surfaces as they move through the surrounding air; such surfaces are called airfoils. A typical airfoil shape is shown in Figure 2.3. Two laws of physics come into play as lift is generated: (1) the air flowing over the curved top of the wing speeds up (for those who care, this is called a "venturi" action), and (2) the faster-flowing air creates a lower pressure over the wing top surfaces. The air passing beneath the wing's relatively flat bottom flows more slowly than that on top; a higher pressure results. With low pressure above, high pressure below, and other aerodynamic effects, the wing tends to move upward as lift is developed (see Figure 2.4).

Figure 2.3. Airfoil (wing) cross-section.

Figure 2.4. Airflow past wing.

CONTROL OF THE FOUR FACTORS

The pilot controls, through his or her power, or thrust, levers and by manipulating various control surfaces built into the plane's wings and tail, the four forces that are involved in flying.

Takeoff

Power (thrust) moves the airplane faster and faster until there is enough airflow over the wings to generate enough lift to overcome the weight. At the proper speed, the pilot uses "elevators" to lift off the ground. Elevators are movable portions of the plane's tail surfaces that control up or down motion (see Figure 2.5).

Descent

The pilot reduces power; drag slows the airplane. With less airflow over the wings, there is less lift generated, and the gravity overcomes the lift. The pilot controls the steepness of the descent with the elevators.

Thrust versus lift

The pilot increases or decreases power with his engine, increasing and decreasing speed, thereby increasing and decreasing the amount of lift that's generated. The speed and flight path (climb, level, descent) are controlled by the pilot's coordination of thrust levers and elevators.

Some of the drag of the airplane moving through the air can't be changed, but some of it can by the lowering or raising of wing flaps into the airstream. When wing flaps are first lowered (as for takeoff), they increase drag a little but also increase lift. After takeoff they're raised, streamlining the wing. When the plane is preparing for approach and landing, flaps are lowered progressively until maximum drag and reduced power reduce speed for landing.

The wing flaps, mounted on the trailing or rear edge of the wings, are extended in various increments to increase lift or drag as required. Some aircraft have similar leading edge devices mounted on the front of the wings. Panels on top of the wings are raised at times during flight as "speed

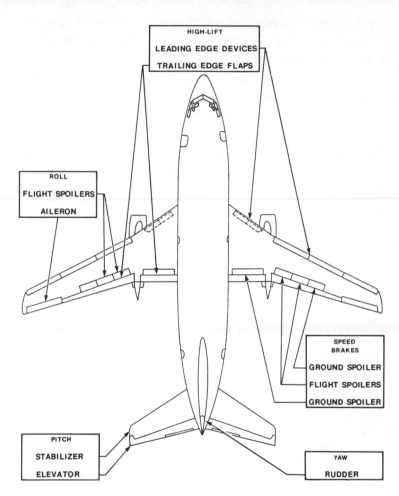

HIGH-LIFT

LEADING EDGE DEVICES

TRAILING EDGE FLAPS

ROLL

FLIGHT SPOILERS

AILERON

SPEED BRAKES

GROUND SPOILER

FLIGHT SPOILERS

GROUND SPOILER

PITCH

STABILIZER

ELEVATOR

YAW

RUDDER

Figure 2.5. Control surfaces.

brakes." After landing, the same panels are raised; they're called "spoilers" at this time (they "spoil" the lift of the wings). The airplane now rests more heavily on the ground; this makes wheel braking more effective (more of the rubber tire is gripping the paved runway surface).

The control of the airplane itself, using the four factors, is accomplished by the moving of various panels, or surfaces, into the airstream, diverting the airplane's path. It climbs or descends with the moving of elevator panels into the airstream, causing the aircraft nose to move up or down. Aileron panels on each wing allow the airplane to bank in one direction or the other (example: right wing down or right wing up). A rudder is turned right or left into the airstream, causing the airplane's nose to move right or left. The aileron and the rudder actions are coordinated by the pilot to make a smooth, banked turn.

Planes are designed and built to be inherently stable. If the pilot took his or her hands and feet off the controls, the airplane would continue on its same path (for instance, level flight) until moved from it by some outside force, such as wind gusts. Even then, since the airplane is inherently stable, it will eventually level itself again.

A Thought to Fly by

Airplanes are inherently stable and can fly "hands off."

WHAT IS AN AIRPLANE STALL?

If the wing or airfoil is tilted up too sharply, with not enough thrust or with too much drag, the formerly smooth airflow over the top of the wing "burbles," and lift is decreased. The wing then "stalls," and the leading edge tilts down to allow thrust and gravity to increase airspeed enough to again create lift from a swift airflow over the wing. The airplane is again "flying." (See Figure 2.6.)

The "tilt down" normally is accomplished by the pilot, but the plane will do it by itself if left to its own devices.

Student pilots learn about this in their first hours of instruction; they learn quickly to ignore Grandma's advice to "fly low and slow."

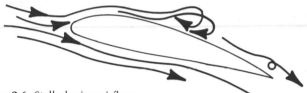

Figure 2.6. Stalled wing airflow.

WHAT IS "FLYING BY THE NUMBERS"?

An airliner's takeoff (and landing) is scientifically structured so that the pilot makes it "by the numbers." The numbers are established by taking into consideration the wind, temperature, airport elevation, and other factors— especially weight.

With the takeoff weight known, the pilot computes velocity values—V1, Vr, and V2. Those three speeds are then prominently displayed in the cockpit, and the takeoff run is begun. The pilot "not flying" calls out the V speeds as they are reached.

The first, V1, is a decision speed; if anything out of the ordinary occurs—a light or bell signal, an instrument indication—and the airplane has not reached V1 speed, the pilot stops. The pilot rejects the takeoff; by operating by the computed performance numbers, there will be enough runway remaining on which to stop. Almost any indication of something not 100 percent right is enough to cause an aborted takeoff.

If V1 speed has been reached or exceeded when the indication occurs—even if a powerplant has failed—the pilot will continue the takeoff. When the pilot accelerates to Vr speed, he or she "rotates" the nose upward with the elevators, lifts the plane off the ground, and climbs upward at the V2 speed previously computed from a chart. This airspeed is a safe, efficient speed to fly with a failed engine. The pilot now either returns to land at the airport from which the plane just took off, or, if weather conditions are not suitable, he or she could continue on to and land at a specified alternate airport.

The airplane's landing approach also is flown by the numbers computed according to its weight. The weight is, of course, lighter than on takeoff because much of the fuel has been consumed.

We know that there is concern about how the plane can fly straight with an inoperative engine on one side of the plane. Won't it turn in that direction? The pilot positions "trim" devices on the control surfaces so that the plane will fly straight ahead.

AUTOPILOT CONTROL

Quite often, possibly 70 percent of the time in the air, the plane's progress is being controlled by the aircraft's auto flight system. Upon hearing this, some of you fearful flyers have said, "Well, that allows the pilots to read their newspapers." What a negative reaction that is! The *positive* fact of the matter is that the pilot now has more time to monitor other aspects of the flight, to preview procedures for the next approach and landing, to talk to the passengers on the P.A. system, and so on.

An example of how the autopilot helps the human pilot fly the airplane: The captain of a flight is adhering to a certain compass heading, a certain airspeed, and a certain altitude. He or she can do these quite well, but there is a certain amount of concentration involved. The pilot turns on the autopilot; it can monitor these givens as well as the pilot can, perhaps even better. But *it* doesn't have to concentrate; *it* doesn't get even a little bit tired. Even so, it's not left to its own devices. It is continually monitored during use by the pilots and by indication and warning systems.

The autopilot can accomplish much more. It can turn to desired compass headings, it can make climbs and descents, and it can hold selected speeds. On command it can fly the airplane so as to intercept and fly along a selected navigational course. (If your automobile had a similar "autodriver," you could command it to drive east along Route 30 and, when reaching Route 88 north, turn left and stay in the right-hand lane.) One of the best things the autopilot does is help to make an instrument approach to an airport runway when the cloud ceiling and the visibility are quite low. A typical low cloud height is 200 feet above the ground with visibility of one-half mile.

Today's pilots command superb airplanes with sophisticated avionics systems and super-sophisticated computers that can do much of the flying automatically, safely, and efficiently. The pilots use these aids, but they still also like to make their own instrument approaches and their own landings—even if they aren't *always* made as smoothly as the autopilot can make them. Autopilots are a plus in today's flying, not a negative.

A BRIEF SUMMARY

Most fearful flyers have misconceptions and misunderstandings about how safely airplanes fly with and without engines. We learned that planes don't fly suspended in empty space; instead, they're well supported in a solid ocean of air. The forces acting on airplanes in flight are easily understandable and reassuring. There is no magic involved. Those "fearsome" noises of flight that worry people are simply normal flight sounds and shouldn't be feared. We also learned that automatic pilots help human pilots fly the airplanes safely and efficiently.

CHAPTER 3

Why Are They So Fearful?

The fear of flying is often referred to as *aviophobia* or *aerophobia*. People aren't born with this fear; they learn it somewhere along the way. Remember, humans are born with only two fears, the fear of falling and the fear of loud noises. But most of us develop other fears or phobias as we go through life.

According to the Boeing study referred to earlier, 25 million Americans are afraid to fly. Do these people have a fear or a phobia, and what is the difference between the two? And does it matter anyway?

Webster's defines a fear as "an unpleasant, often strong emotion caused by anticipation or awareness of danger." Synonyms are: *dread, fright, alarm, panic, terror,* and *trepidation. Phobia* is defined as "an exaggerated, usually inexplicable and illogical fear of a particular object or class of objects."[1] *Phobia* comes from the Greek word *phobas,* meaning flight, fear, or dread. The difference between a fear and a phobia seems to be that fearful people are reacting to a real danger, whereas phobics are exaggerating the danger, and their fears are usually inexplicable or illogical.

Many people have a fear of snakes. A fear of snakes may seem to be a logical fear and not a phobia, but according to the dictionary definition, it's logical only if there's some real danger involved. If we put a man who has a fear of snakes into a room with several uncaged snakes, he would most likely want out! Even if we assured him that the snakes were nonpoisonous and completely harmless, he would still want out. Does he have a fear or a phobia? It seems impossible to tell where one leaves off and the other begins. The important factor is how much the fear or phobia is distressing you and how much it is interfering with your life.

HOW FEARS AND PHOBIAS DEVELOP

Freudian theory

Freudians contend that a phobia is really a displacement of anxiety from an original fearful object or situation to another object or situation. This psychoanalytical concept is based largely on Sigmund Freud's case history in 1909 of little Hans. Hans was a five-year-old boy who was terrified of horses. Freud felt that the boy was not really afraid of horses but of his father; he feared that his father would castrate him because he was sexually attracted to his mother. Hans unconsciously felt it was safer to be afraid of horses than to admit to a fear of his own father.[2]

Freud was convinced that phobias develop in adults who have disturbed sexual relationships and who have failed to resolve their Oedipal problems. The treatment for this can be long and complex. It may involve years of psychoanalysis, using free association and/or dream interpretation. Freud also believed that clearing up the phobia would do no good because it was only a symptom of an underlying problem. In fact, he felt that if you cleared up the phobia or symptom, another fear would replace it.

In our work with more than 2,000 fearful flyers, we have never seen this happen. Not only have 97 percent of them overcome their fear of flying, but many have used the same methods to overcome other fears.

Certainly, fearful flyers may have other problems they need to work on and may benefit from psychotherapy or analysis, but behavioral methods seem to work better than traditional psychotherapy to cure the fear of flying. We often get people in our classes who have tried other methods with limited or no success.

Behavioral theory

Behaviorists believe that phobias are learned or conditioned responses. According to this theory, a person may develop a phobia as the result of a single painful or frightening experience. And the individual almost certainly will develop one if the initial fear is intense or if the traumatic experience is repeated many times. The fear may then generalize to similar objects or situations.

In 1920, John B. Watson, a psychologist, and his assistant proved that phobias can be learned. They did an experiment with a young child, Albert, who was not afraid of white rats but was afraid of loud noises. They proceeded to pair the introduction of a white rat with a loud noise. Each time they showed Albert the white rat, they made a sudden loud noise. Not only did Albert become afraid of the white rat, but after a while, the psychologists did not even have to make the loud noise, and the boy was still afraid of the rat. The fear then began to generalize to all furry objects.[3] (Such an experiment would be considered unethical today.)

A student of ours, Joe, developed his fear of flying in a similar way. After he received a war injury, the army flew him back to the States on an army transport plane, flat on his back on a stretcher. During the long flight home, Joe worried about many things. What would his family think when they saw him? Would he recover? Would he be able to return to work? He felt very anxious and "stressed" during the flight.

Joe did recover from his injury, and he was able to return to work. But an odd thing happened: He no longer liked to fly. His fear became so intense that he hadn't flown for more than thirty years when he came to our class. The stress and anxiety about his condition and his family that he experienced on that trip home became paired up with airplanes and flying.

Barbara developed her fear while flying to her father's funeral. During the long flight, she was anxious and depressed. She felt guilty and regretful that she had not been able to see her father before he died. Her body became tense, and she developed other physical symptoms of anxiety. Subsequently, whenever she tried to fly, she became anxious and depressed. She eventually stopped flying altogether.

A Thought to Fly by

If you're anxious about something (your job, marriage, health) while you're flying, that anxiety may become paired up with the airplane.

Role modeling

A person might develop a phobia by being exposed to a faulty role model. If your mother was afraid of thunderstorms and took you and your siblings and hid in a closet every time it rained, you might well develop a fear of thunderstorms. You might even develop a fear of closets.

Dan's mother was afraid of everything—especially airplanes. She had no reason or opportunity to fly, so she did not have to deal with her fear. If there was an airline accident, she talked endlessly about it and said, "See, I told you it was dangerous!" When Dan grew up, he had many opportunities to fly, but he was too fearful to attempt it. He could still hear his mother's voice, espousing the danger of it.

Lack of knowledge

A person may have a frightening experience while flying. If an individual were on a turbulent flight and thought that the airplane was going to come apart or fall out of the sky, he or she might become anxious. During a subsequent flight, there might not be any turbulence at all, but this individual might be frightened just waiting for some turbulence to occur or just remembering the last time. A person may hear a strange noise while flying and worry that something is happening to the airplane. This strange noise may just be that of the landing gear being lowered, but it may also be enough to make a timid flyer even more anxious.

Secondary gains

Fearful flyers must ask themselves if they are gaining something by *not* flying. They certainly do not have to put up with those terrible physical symptoms if they do not fly, but are there other gains also? One young woman told us that she was upset that she couldn't fly with her husband and children to Florida each winter. Her in-laws lived there and expected them to visit for two weeks each year. We later learned that these visits were very stressful for her; she disliked her domineering mother-in-law and felt that she could do nothing to please her. By not flying, phobics may get sympathy, attention, control over others, and freedom from doing things they really don't want to do.

OVERCOMING YOUR FEARS AND PHOBIAS

In 1924, another psychologist, Mary Cover Jones, did an experiment to show that conditioning can also cure fears.[4] Her subject was a three-year-old boy who was already afraid of furry objects. She introduced a white rabbit in a wire cage, at the end of the room while the boy was eating (a pleasurable experience). Each day, the rabbit was moved closer to the boy until he could eat with one hand while petting the rabbit with the other. Not only did he no longer fear rabbits but he also lost his fear of white rats and rugs.

We are going to show you how to pair up relaxation (a pleasurable experience) with an airplane. This will enable you to feel comfortable on an airplane. Remember: You weren't born with the fear of flying, you learned it somewhere along the way.

A Thought to Fly by

Anything learned can be unlearned.

Our hope is that you have gained some insight into how you developed your fear of flying. But even if you still don't know how you became afraid or even what you're afraid of, the relaxation exercises, thought-stopping techniques, and aviation education in this book will help you overcome your fear (or phobia?).

CHAPTER 4

The Winds, the Weather, and the Wheres and Whys of Turbulence

Flyers who worry about flying worry about weather. They worry about obvious bad weather like thunderstorms, tornados, lightning, and sleet. But they also worry about rain, about clouds, and about wind (there are all kinds of winds, including jetstreams and wind shear).

Turbulence is a big subject. Personal experiences of encounters with rough air, other people's accounts, and media stories, combined with a vivid imagination, can turn an otherwise pleasurable flight into a personal nightmare. Or they might keep someone—might keep you—off airplanes altogether.

People hate turbulence for a number of reasons. First, they're not comfortable while the airplane is bouncing around. They can't eat or drink, or they may spill something on themselves or on others. Worse, they're afraid the airplane might suffer structural damage, might even lose its wings. They're afraid that the pilots might lose control of the airplane.

Do pilots also hate turbulence?

They do. But they don't fear it. They know that the airplane will not break, that it won't lose a wing or suffer other structural damage. And pilots know that they won't lose control of the plane. But they don't like turbulence because they know that when they're in it, they aren't giving their passengers and other crew members the smooth, pleasant flight everyone wants. They don't like it because it can affect their schedules. If it's lasting and it's more than light in intensity, pilots slow down to a "turbulence penetration speed" (which differs for different aircraft). The slowed plane takes the big bumps more easily. Like a fast speedboat clipping through choppy waves tops, if it is slowed down, its passage through water is eased.

Can we assume, then, that
flight attendants also hate turbulence?

Yes. They too know that their passengers may be uncomfortable, if not downright frightened. The choppiness may interfere with smooth and efficient cabin service —a special annoyance if the flight is a short one. Attendants worry that hot or cold drinks may spill on someone. They're also subject to the risks of moving about the cabin in turbulence while making sure that their passengers are complying with the "Fasten Seat Belt" sign.

Could anyone possibly enjoy turbulence?

There are those who actually say they do like it at times. These are generally the same people who enjoy the swaying and swooping rides in amusement parks. It's interesting to note that the slight movement of our bodies experiencing turbulence in flight can't compare with the substantial body movement on roller coasters and swinging chairs. But the minds of fearful flyers are tuned in to the plane's slightest movement. A gentle, banked turn or a slight increase in the climb angle, physical movements that wouldn't be noticed in a train, truck, car, or even a bicycle, can cause anxiety in fearful flyers.

THE BUMPS AND GRINDS
OF ROUGH AIR IN LOWER LEVELS

To ease your mind, let's look at why the air gets bumpy. Understanding the ocean of air in which we fly is extremely helpful. We can liken smooth air to a pond of smooth water. If we throw a cork into the water, it makes ripples, which spread out. The cork rises and falls with the ripples it made or with ripples from another source: a thrown stone or a stream of water flowing into the otherwise calm pond. As the water is agitated by whatever means, a cork or a boat will move up and down or sideways. Likewise, an airplane tends to move with the ripples of air. The difference is that we say it *tends* to; the pilot probably won't let it! The pilot controls the airplane to keep it on the path that has been set.

Most turbulence at low altitudes is caused either by relatively high winds, relatively high temperatures, or both. We'll see that low-level rough air can be caused by strong winds blowing over the earth's surface. If it's blowing over flatlands or over a wide expanse of water, there's little effect.

AIR IS A FLUID—WIND STIRS IT

When winds, especially gusty winds, blow across terrain that has hills and valleys and encounter tall buildings and other obstructions, the ocean of air is agitated and stirred up. If a plane is flying a few hundred feet above the ground, it tends to rise as the wind flows up over protruding buildings; it tends to sink as the wind flows down into low spots; and it wants to rise again at the next hill. The airplane *tends* to rise and fall; it *wants* to ascend and descend. But the pilot wants the airplane to fly in a straight line whether it's climbing, level, or descending, and so our human pilot or the autopilot controls it to do so. Actually, the plane is probably flying so fast through the up urges and the down urges that it doesn't have time to rise or fall, it just bumps! It bumps along like it's driving on a country road, or it rocks and rolls a little as if it were a boat speeding through choppy water.

If you were on an airliner taxiing out for takeoff during this wind condition, the captain would probably announce, "Folks, we expect to encounter a little light chop on our climbout. It'll smooth out in a few minutes, and we expect a smooth flight at our cruising altitude." A captain preparing to land might announce, "Ladies and gentlemen, we expect some light chop, some light turbulence, as we descend into the airport. Make sure your seat belts are tightly fastened."

Since this type of turbulence is caused at lower altitudes by the wind flowing over uneven terrain, it tends to smooth out as altitude increases. Of course, over mountains a plane would have to be comparatively high before the bumps gave way to a smooth ride.

UNEVEN HEATING OF THE SURFACE

Another type of turbulence is also found mostly at lower elevations, but it may also be felt at higher altitudes. This type of bumpiness is caused by uneven heating of the earth's surface and usually dissipates once the plane rises above most cloud formations.

The sun beats down on the earth, heating it up as the day progresses. There is a difference in the way the sun's rays and resultant heat are reflected from the earth's surface. We know that there is a difference even from the coloring of the surface. For instance, light-colored shingles on a roof reflect the heat of the sun's rays and keep the house cooler. Conversely, black or dark gray shingles absorb the sun's rays, and the house stays warmer. Differences in ground surface affect reflectivity also.

To understand how this affects your flight, let's picture a light training airplane on a gliding approach to a concrete runway (see Figure 4.1). The flight instructor explains to the young student, "See that plowed field just ahead of us? You'll find that we'll get an updraft over that field. The plane will want to rise. Don't let it. Maintain this glide angle." Sure enough, the plane starts to rise with the ascending current of air, but the student dutifully applies forward pressure on the control wheel, and they continue the glide. But now the instructor says, "When we get over that green alfalfa field right ahead of us, the plane will try to sink—there'll be a descending air current. Don't let the plane sink." Sure enough, the plane attempts to follow the down current over the alfalfa field. Now they reach the runway end; the instructor predicts that the plane will "balloon" upward as heated air rises from the sunny concrete.

Even a heavy airliner tends to rise and sink with the currents, just as the small trainer did, but at the speeds at which it is flying through ups and downs, there isn't time for

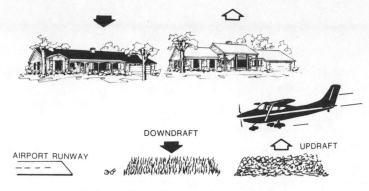

Figure 4.1. Small plane affected by up and down currents.

it to go up or go down as it hits each vertical current. The result is bumps. There might be an up current affecting the nose portion of the airplane at the same time a down current is at the tail portion. And there could be an up current acting on the left wing and a down current at the right wing tip—and moments later all are reversed. And then there are sideways effects, too. There is nothing particularly dangerous about this in flight. It just means that the pilot is busier keeping the airplane flying on the course and at the altitude he or she—or Airway Traffic Control—has selected. The young student pilot we observed landing started learning to fly an airplane through turbulence as well as smooth air within the first few hours of instruction.

The surface temperature of a wide expanse of water is much more constant than an equivalent land mass. Accordingly, a flight over an ocean would normally be smoother than a coast-to-coast land flight, unless turbulence is caused by conditions that we'll explore shortly.

SOME COMFORTING INFORMATION
ON HOW A PLANE FLIES

Any airplane is inherently stable. If a pilot released hands and feet from the controls, the craft would continue to fly just as it was—let's assume straight and level—until disturbed by an outside force such as a wind gust. As an example, a rising current of air lifts the left wing tip and causes the airplane to bank to the right: right wing tilted down, left wing tilted up. If the pilot did not take back control, the airplane would return to level flight on its own because of its stable nature. The same would be true if the nose were displaced downward by a downdraft; with no input from the pilot, the airplane would eventually return to level flight.

CLOUDS, TURBULENCE, AND THUNDERSTORMS

Turbulence is minimal in the morning and maximum in the late afternoon because it is the sun's heat that creates the turbulence. As a strong up current rises, the air cools. That parcel of air contains a certain amount of invisible water vapor. It climbs and cools, and the parcel can no longer hold all of the water vapor. It releases the vapor in the form of visible moisture, and a cloud forms. The release process generates heat, the heat gives the shaft a new lease on life, and it continues rising. The type of cloud formed in this manner is known as cumuliform. The cloud itself is a cumulus—a puffy, pretty white cloud. There are usually a number of them scattered around, each marking rising currents of air.

Many people say, "This is the kind of weather I like to fly in—blue skies, fluffy white clouds." However, flying near large clouds of this type can subject passengers to those updrafts and the accompanying downdrafts. When we have vertical air currents in the atmosphere, we say that the air is unstable.

Air composed mostly of horizontal currents is termed stable. Clouds formed in stable air are flatter, layered clouds called stratus.

We're not saying that you shouldn't fly when there are puffy white clouds; in fact, the very small cumuliform clouds are sometimes called "fair weather" cumulus. The tops are reasonably low, and smooth air can be found just above them. But we are saying that, if the only thing you're looking for is a smooth flight, you'll find it on a day when clouds are low, flat, and gray and when a fine drizzle is falling almost straight down.

With this condition, your plane will climb quickly through the clouds, and you'll probably—not always, but probably—break out into brilliant sunshine with blue skies above. Those gray-bottomed clouds will be bright white on top; you'll think you're flying over a field of snow.

In the late afternoon, that fluffy white cloud may take on a more ominous appearance. If it grows in size and has a gleaming white top, but the base becomes blue-gray, we call this a cumulo-nimbus cloud. It now may be a fully developed thunderstorm. The blue-gray hue is a sign of rain, and where there's moisture in unstable air, there may be turbulence.

Flying directly beneath that thunderstorm, we would encounter swiftly rising updrafts. All around the updrafts, though, the air spills over and creates swiftly descending downdrafts. There could be areas of heavy rain, and hail can be encountered. There may be lightning also, cloud to cloud, or cloud to ground. (Fortunately, storms like this are prominently "painted" on weather radar and can be avoided most of the time.) Later, as the storm begins to dissipate, the cloud fans out on top—it looks like an anvil (see Figure 4.2). This thundercloud could be alone, could merge with others, or could even form a line of thunderstorms.

CUMULO NIMBUS CLOUD   STRATUS CLOUD

Figure 4.2. Cumulus and stratus cloud forms.

Airliners avoid flying through thunderstorms whenever possible, usually skirting them by at least twenty miles. What happens if they have to be penetrated to climb out of a departure point or descend to a landing? Takeoffs or landings should not be made when a thunderstorm of moderate intensity is in progress at or approaching the airport. When a thunderstorm—or a line of them—must be flown through, the plane's weather radar picks the path through the areas containing the least moisture and thus the smoothest route. If weather radar on an airliner is inoperative, the pilot must fly a route on which there are no thunderstorms. Air Traffic Control's (ATC) weather radar can also help planes fly smoother paths in thunderstorm areas, although its main radar function is to provide traffic separation. The airliner's radar primarily provides storm avoidance and some ground mapping—the scope shows coast lines or mountain ranges—it does not indicate other air traffic.

Much of our turbulence occurs in or near clouds that contain a lot of moisture, and the moisture is what shows up on weather radar. As we started flying higher with jets, we found Clear Air Turbulence (CAT). Part of CAT's definition is "atmospheric turbulence which is not visibly apparent to the naked eye." That means that there's not enough moisture there for clouds to form and be seen; therefore, there's not enough to be painted on radar. CAT occurs with a significant change in wind speed and is actually a wind shear situation. You'll read later in this chapter that wind shear is a phenomenon that is hazardous only at low levels in the atmosphere. However, an unforeseen encounter with CAT at high flight levels could cause injury to people who aren't in their seats with seat belts fastened. This is why flight attendants will often announce, "The captain has turned off the seat belt sign. Feel free to move about the cabin. However, we suggest that when you're in your seat, you keep your seat belt fastened about you. We can't always predict turbulence." CAT is not any more dangerous than any other type of turbulence is, so long as belts are fastened. There are no "air pockets" in the atmosphere, only rising, descending, and cross-currents of air.

Interaction of the air masses can also produce turbulence in our ocean of air at higher as well as lower altitudes. Just as two different flowing bodies of water meeting together may bubble and burble, boil and roil, so will two dissimilar, meeting air masses. In both cases, they may be different by temperature, height, direction of movement, velocity of the winds, amount of moisture, or any combination of these. Many people have become familiar with terms such as "cold front," "warm front," "low-pressure area," "high-pressure area," and others. All these involve different air masses meeting, with one overriding another, or one burrowing under another, or just bumping together sideways. Whatever the reasons for the meetings of these masses, the resulting stirred-up air provides ripples or waves or sometimes whirlpools through which planes must pass. Or, if flight conditions are too turbulent, policies, pilot, or dispatcher judgment will dictate that the area be avoided, or that a flight must actually be canceled. Again, a plane encountering air turbulence can be likened to a car traveling country roads or city potholes, generally for just a short time.

A Thought to Fly by

Your body is not subjected to as much moving or jolting in air turbulence as it is in an automobile ride on rough roads.

Worried flyers worry more when they hear about jetstreams, the high-velocity, high-altitude rivers of wind that normally flow from west to east in the United States.

These are not dangerous. But, like the stream that flows into an otherwise placid pond, jetstreams can create the conditions that cause turbulence, such as high-level thunderstorms. Other high-altitude wind phenomena also are not dangerous, including even the one that has become notorious—wind shear. High-velocity, fast-shifting winds are something to be aware of near the ground, but they are not particular problems "at altitude."

AIRLINE PILOTS COOPERATE FOR COMFORT

You've learned that pilots don't like turbulence—they want you to have a comfortable flight. This means all pilots, regardless of the airline they fly for. Airlines' advertising and marketing people fight their competitors right down to the last passenger. But in the air, pilots, in conjunction with ATC, discuss flight conditions and offer suggestions for altitude or routing changes that will result in smoother travel.

Thoughts to Fly by

You don't have to like turbulence. You don't even have to feel comfortable with it. But it won't hurt you, and it won't hurt the airplane. This assumes that you are in your seat with your seat belt fastened.

OTHER WEATHER

Let's consider other weather conditions commonly feared by fearful flyers. Rain does not affect an aircraft's flight or engine operation as long as proscribed procedures are used. It can restrict visibility during takeoffs and landings. Certain minimum visibilities are specified for these occasions.

Ceiling height—the height of the base of the lowest broken or overcast clouds—also has a specific minimum value for safe takeoffs and landings.

A flight may descend in cloud conditions that prevent pilots from seeing the world outside their windshield. Using approved instrument approach systems (electronics) and approach procedures (displayed on cockpit charts), the descent is made to a minimum altitude specified on the approach chart. At that point, if visibility is as reported and the runway or associated lights are in view, the plane is landed. Otherwise, the captain makes or commands a "go around" or missed approach maneuver. He or she then elects to either fly to an alternate airport or make another approach. Rain can also be a factor during takeoffs and landings if it causes water standing on runways to exceed specified depths. These minimum specifications are legal safety factors that must be (and are) observed.

The intensity of freezing rain—if moderate or greater—can prohibit takeoffs and landings. *Light* freezing rain (or drizzle) is okay for all operations. Snow in the atomosphere is no problem for takeoff, flight, or landing, except as it affects visibility during takeoff and landing. However, snow on runways or on an airplane can be an operational problem. Its allowable depth on runways varies as to whether it's dry or wet snow. (Wet snow, slush, and standing water have the same limits.) The limit for allowable snow—or ice—on the airplane during takeoff is zero.

Airline pilots and dispatchers ask three questions about their operations in wintertime conditions:

1. What's on the airplane?
2. What's on the runway?
3. What are we doing about it?

Every fearful flyer vividly remembers the Air Florida Boeing 737 crash in 1982 in Washington's Potomac River. The plane's flight crew erred in attempting to take off with snow and ice adhering to the aircraft structure. The principal problem was not the ice and snow's weight; instead, frozen contaminant on wings and tail surfaces disturbed the smooth flow of air around those airfoils, and lifting ability was reduced. A few paragraphs back we said that rain does not affect engine operation if proscribed procedures are used. This is true for snow and ice as well.

That crew committed another basic blunder by not turning on the engines' anti-ice systems for takeoff. A resultant lack of heat to de-ice an important engine air probe caused pilots' engine instruments to lie, indicating that the engines were producing maximum takeoff power when they were actually far below that value. One more blunder was that the erroneous readings—one for each engine—were accepted and not checked, and other power instruments, which had to be saying, "The EPR [engine pressure ratio] gauges are incorrect," were not believed. (See Figure 4.3.)

*How could an airline put a crew
like that on a plane?*

This was really a one-in-a-billion situation. Those pilots were relatively well qualified and trained but also were inexperienced in winter flying. They evidently didn't believe all those things they had been taught about the effects of ice and snow on the airplane during takeoff. In flight, modern anti-icing and de-icing systems keep wings

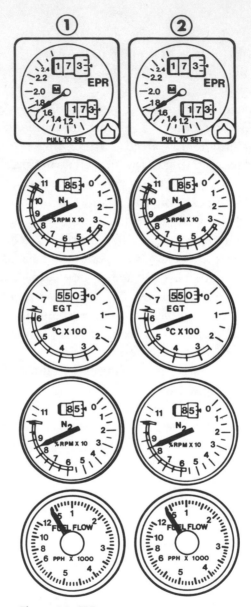

Figure 4.3. EPR gauges (top row).

and windshields, engines and antennae free of ice. But, before departure, all vital parts are sprayed with a de-icing fluid, and they may also be brushed and scraped. The captain is responsible for seeing that his or her plane is *clean* for every takeoff.

There has never been an accident or serious incident in air travel from which some good didn't result. Since the 1982 Air Florida accident, much, much more emphasis has been put on cold-weather operations by government agencies, airlines, and all other aviation organizations worldwide. Winter flying was safe before; it's even safer today because of that accident.

TAKEOFFS ARE NOT DANGEROUS

The Washington National Airport accident occurred during takeoff. Some months later, another accident occurred during a takeoff in New Orleans, and countless fearful flyers decided that takeoffs are dangerous. Two accidents just months apart helped convince many people that they shouldn't fly.

But if we look at it another way, we find thirty-four months in which there were only two takeoff accidents. During this period, one airline alone—USAir—was making 1,000 completely safe takeoffs every day! All the airlines of the United States were making 14,000 completely safe takeoffs daily. In that thirty-four-month period, *this totaled fourteen million, two hundred and eighty thousand (14,280,000) completely safe takeoffs.* And some people worry about *two* in that period.*

*Additional takeoff accidents have occurred since those cited here, but the statistical figures are still outstandingly on the safe side. As this is written, U.S. airlines are making more than 17,000 takeoffs daily.

Incidentally, few people seem to remember that there was a fatal accident on Washington's Metro subway system on the same day as the Air Florida accident. Did many people quit riding the Metro for that reason?

OTHER WEATHER SITUATIONS AND THEIR EFFECT—OR NONEFFECT—ON FLIGHT

Fog

Fog is a cloud on the ground. Let's lump smoke in with fog. Smoke and fog can affect visibility, but that's all. If pilots have the required level of visibility, they can take off or land—if not, they cannot.

On a typical low weather condition flight—low cloud ceilings, low (restricted) visibility—the pilots may not have visual contact with the ground until just seconds before touching down on the destination runway. They fly using their electronic navigation systems and navigation instruments. These systems and instruments are used whether or not the pilots can see outside the plane. The pilots, like passengers, like to look at the ground, snow-capped mountains, winding rivers, ocean shores, cities, and beautiful cloud formations. But they fly the flight safely, efficiently, and comfortably, without those pleasant scenes.

Lightning: no worry

Lightning is always discussed during our fearful flyers' courses. Being struck by lightning in a modern airliner is not an item of great concern. Only one fatal accident to an airliner in flight has been documented as caused by lightning. This was in the 1950s and involved a fuel venting system (quickly modified) that allowed accumulated fuel fumes to be ignited by lightning. The Air Force has reported *military* aircraft lost to lightning, though.

In the United States, the Federal Aviation Administration (FAA) regulates the design and building of aircraft. Before the FAA will certify an aircraft for civil service, it must be satisfied that the aircraft is protected against lightning. Today, aircraft are protected by special shielding, insulators, isolators, and grounding techniques. One device visible to passengers is the static discharge wick. A number of these can be seen extending back from the rear edge of the wings and from the vertical and horizontal tail surfaces. They vary in number, length, placement, and color (white, gray, black, or brown). They may remind you of the lightning rods that used to grace barn roofs. Electrical static that builds up in the aircraft structure flows out into the atmosphere by way of these wicks.

The next time you've got a close-up view of the nose of an airliner, notice the radome, a streamlined molded cover over the aircraft's weather radar antenna. Diverter strips are applied to the radome in a pattern that produces minimum interference in the operation of the radar but will protect the antenna by conducting lightning current harmlessly away.

Wind shear

There have been airline accidents attributed to wind shear. Media coverage makes it out to be an even greater danger than it is. Misunderstanding and misinformation abound. For instance, people fear wind shear at high altitudes, but it is only close to the ground that the pilots need to be concerned. True, we say that Clear Air Turbulence

(CAT) is wind shear "at altitude," but we're concerned only with the turbulence aspect of CAT 'way up there, not wind shear.

What *is* wind shear? Its strict definition is a change in wind direction or a change in wind velocity or both, occurring in a short distance (which, in a plane, is a short *time*). There is almost always wind shear in the atmosphere. As airplanes move swiftly through the air ocean and change altitudes, such wind shifts, or shears, are encountered often. This is normal. What does concern us is *severe* wind shear when we're near the ground. There we're concerned about weather phenomena known as downbursts.

Airplanes normally take off and land into the wind. Airplanes can tolerate a certain amount of downwind (wind from behind, on the tail) and a certain amount of crosswind during takeoff and landing, the amount differing with the type of airplane and other factors. For instance, if we were on a flight landing at Washington National and the wind were reported as being from the north at ten miles an hour, we'd probably prefer to land on Runway 36, the north runway.

As we descend, we might find that we actually have a tailwind pushing us forward, instead of a headwind holding us back. It might be blowing at twenty miles an hour. As we descended farther, the wind would change direction— become more of a crosswind—and would drop in velocity. As we neared the ground, the wind would have shifted to a headwind—from the north—and wind speed would have dropped to ten miles per hour. This is a normal occurrence, even though there's wind shear of a sort.

The phenomenon that has given wind shear a bad name is the downburst. The downburst is a fast-descending column of air that hits the ground, spreads out in all directions, and surges upward around the edges. (Its action is easily understood if we direct a stream of water from a garden hose straight toward the ground. It shoots downward and makes an impact at a high velocity; it spreads out in all directions; and the water is deflected upward all around.) A small but intense downburst is called a microburst—it's small in diameter and lasts only about fifteen minutes. It is intense for only about five minutes. Pilots approaching such an occurrence sometimes report rain from below rather than falling from above. It's being carried upward with the deflected-upward airflow. (See Figure 4.4.)

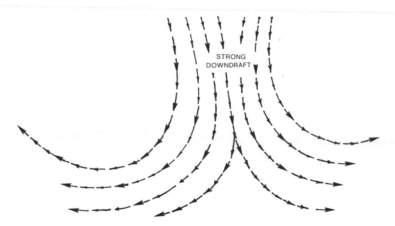

Figure 4.4. Profile of a downburst.

Let's say a flight enters a microburst. As it encounters the outer edges, where the air is now an updraft, the plane tends to rise. As it flies forward into the center, it encounters the downdrafts, and the airplane will want to descend. Now at the far, outer edges, it will again tend to rise with updrafts. Passage through the microburst takes only seconds, as the typical plane is flying then at speeds of 100 to 150 knots.

We talk about the plane's *tending* to rise and *wanting* to descend, and we've said the pilot doesn't let it, because he or she wants to remain on a certain path. And this is the way the plane is flown through similar updraft/downdraft conditions high in the air. But when the plane is either taking off, landing, or going around from an attempted landing, maneuvers for which certain paths must be flown and certain speeds maintained, wind shear may be of some concern.

For example, if a plane is landing, as the updraft is encountered, the plane will tend to rise, and the plane's airspeed will increase. The pilot automatically will reduce power and lower the plane's nose slightly to hold the glide path he or she was following. About the time the proper glideslope was regained and speed was lowered, or lowering, the pilot might encounter the tremendous downdrafts of the microburst. Now the power has to be swiftly increased and the aircraft's nose raised—the pilot needs to hold or increase altitude and needs to increase speed. It is at this critical time that some accidents have occurred; the speed and climb capabilities of the plane were not regained in time.

It wasn't until the turbojet transport came into use that severe downdrafts such as the microbursts were identified. Accidents prior to this merely were blamed on "pilot error." This label still goes onto reports of crashes caused by low-level wind shear; it's a convenient label, and the pilot *is* responsible for the safety and welfare of the plane, its passengers, and its crew. But it has been realized that we really didn't, in the past, understand the forces exerted by downbursts and their effects on airplanes. A vast effort has been made by the worldwide aviation industry to learn more about wind shear and what to do about it. What has been done and what yet is being done should ensure that future airline accidents due to severe wind shear will be few and far between—if there are any at all.

- Flight crews, dispatchers, air-traffic controllers, and meteorologists have been given much training on this weather phenomenon, including how to recognize it, forecast it, communicate its presence, and, thus, avoid it.
- Pilots are given simulator training on actual wind shear situations that have caused accidents. They learn how to fly the airplane so as to minimize the effects of the downburst. Training and operation escape procedures have been developed jointly by the FAA, aircraft manufacturers, and airlines and are being used by airlines and corporate plane operators.
- Airport systems are in place to warn of low-level wind shear hazards. Further development is expanding the capability to give earlier and more precise warning.
- Airborne systems are going into cockpits to give early warning, then information and commands to enable the pilots to safely fly out of the problem area.

Why don't the pilots just stay away from those thunderstorms when wind shear has been predicted?

First, downbursts *can* occur in conjunction with thunderstorms. Probably most of them do. But they can also occur when there is a temperature inversion (air temperature warmer at higher elevations instead of cooler), with warm or cold fronts, or with high surface winds near hill-and-valley airports. If planes didn't fly whenever there was the *slightest chance* of a microburst, air travel would not be the dependable form of transportation that it is today. Airline captains—and airline dispatchers—are paid quite well to exercise good judgment as they plan and operate each phase of each and every flight. And this includes any weather condition that could produce low-level wind shear.

A Thought to Fly by

Airline accidents that are attributed to "weather" still occur, but they're few and far between.

CHAPTER 5

No More Tension . . . Nothing But Relaxation

You can't be tense and relaxed at the same time. It's physiologically impossible. If you can train your body to relax at will, even in anxiety-producing situations, you will be able to fly comfortably. You will be able to control the fear instead of letting it control you and your life. You've learned to be tense and anxious about flying, and your body has learned to respond in a certain way.

> **A Thought to Fly by**
>
> Anything learned can be unlearned, including your bodily responses to fear.

Progressive relaxation methods will enable you to get rid of the tension and relax your body. Relaxing your body will help you overcome your fear of flying. Even though the fear seems to be in your mind, your mental and physical conditions are so closely connected that one affects the other. No matter which one you work on first, the other will be affected.

BODILY RESPONSES
TO FEAR

When you feel anxious or threatened, physical changes take place in your body. Your pupils enlarge, your hearing becomes more acute, blood drains from your extremities, your muscles shorten and contract, and your heart and respiratory rates increase. This is called the "fight or flight" response. We inherited it from our ancestors, and it was an appropriate response to many of the situations they found themselves in. Our ancestors lived in caves and had to hunt for food and fight off wild animals. They needed extra adrenaline and all of their senses to be on the alert. And we sometimes need this response today. But often, we signal our bodies to be on the alert when it isn't appropriate. We tend to use the "fight or flight" response to meet deadlines at the office or while sitting in traffic jams.

Many of us walk around tense and alert most of the day and aren't even aware of it. Maybe we grew up in a home where there was a lot of tension, and so we *learned* to be tense and anxious. It became our natural way of responding and a part of our everyday posture. It may no longer be appropriate, but we may not recognize what we are doing, let alone know how to change it.

If you are a fearful flyer, you activate the "fight or flight" response when you fly or even think about flying. If it's a long fight, your body may be on the alert for hours. No wonder fearful flyers are exhausted by the time they reach their destination.

Let's look more closely at three of your body's systems and see what happens when they are on the alert for too long.

Neuromuscular system

You will often feel tension first in your muscles. They shorten and contract; the muscles along the back of your neck, shoulders, arms, and hands, in particular, may feel tight and constricted. Your shoulders may be hunched up toward your ears. After a while, muscular aches and pains, headaches, and backaches may develop. It is these muscle tightenings that you experience as tension and that are connected to your feelings of anxiety. You can lower the anxiety by eliminating this tension through progressive relaxation.

Cardiovascular system

Fear can cause heart palpitations. Your heart may seem to miss a beat or feel as if it is beating so hard that it's going to come right through your chest wall. Your heart rate can increase to as many as 200 to 300 beats per minute instead of an average of 70 beats per minute. Progressive relaxation can slow down a rapid heartbeat.

Respiratory system

Shortness of breath and hyperventilation may occur when you are anxious. Your breathing may become faster (or more shallow). Eventually, this type of breathing eliminates much of the oxygen in the lungs, and the carbon dioxide builds up. When this occurs, you feel short of breath and begin to breathe even more quickly. This will cause the imbalance to become more severe, and you may experience dizziness, chest pains, numbness in the hands and body, and impaired vision. Progressive relaxation can slow down your breathing.

Progressive relaxation treats anxiety directly. As you learn to relax your muscles, you will reverse the "fight or flight" response and return your body to its natural, balanced state. Not only will your muscles relax, but your heartbeat and breathing also will return to normal.

THE ANXIETY CYCLE

Most of you have experienced some or all of the physical symptoms of fear discussed in Chapter 1. These physical symptoms compound your fear and start a vicious cycle. This is the anxiety cycle. First you are afraid. Then you get a few physical symptoms, which make you more fearful. Now, you start to worry if you're going to have a heart attack or faint. This makes you more anxious, which increases the intensity of the physical symptoms, which increases the anxiety—and on it goes in an ever-worsening cycle.

The anxiety cycle starts at a low level, but it keeps escalating. If you don't stop or interrupt this cycle when it first begins or when it is still at a low level, the anxiety will continue to gain momentum until you feel overwhelmed and panicky. But if you had a tool that could break into that cycle before the anxiety starts or when it is still at a low level, it would mean that you would never get to the point where you felt out of control, overwhelmed, or panicky. You would always have this tool with you, you would know how to use it effectively, and it would always work. Sound too good to be true? Actually, we are going to show you two methods that are each a powerful tool to combat anxiety. They are *progressive relaxation* and a cognitive therapy called *thought stopping*.

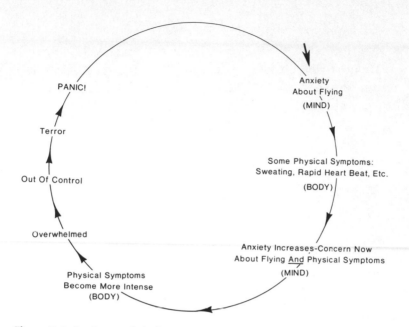

Figure 5.1. Anxiety cycle before progressive relaxation training.

If you can relax your body before you get into a fearful situation or when you first begin to feel anxious, you will not get those horrible uncomfortable feelings. Even if you can stop the anxiety for only a few minutes, it will lose its power and momentum. It will have to start all over and at a lower level.

A Thought to Fly by

You can't be tense and relaxed at the same time.

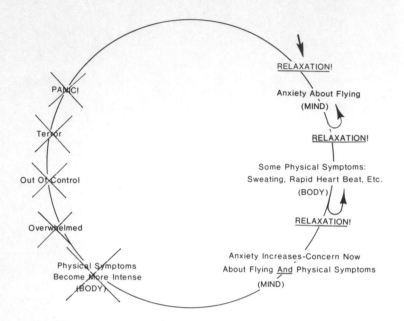

Figure 5.2. Anxiety cycle after progressive relaxation training.

PROGRESSIVE RELAXATION AND YOUR PHOBIA

If you have claustrophobia, a fear of heights, or a fear of not being in control, you may wonder how relaxation is going to help. But remember, it's the physical symptoms of fear that make you so uncomfortable. If you don't get any of these physical symptoms (tenseness, rapid heartbeat, difficulty breathing), then the anxiety cycle will not start. You will never feel out of control, overwhelmed, or panicky. Progressive relaxation can help you feel comfortable, even on an airplane. But you can't learn this overnight. You have to practice many weeks before you can use this technique in a fear-provoking situation.

Progressive relaxation

The principle behind the relaxation exercises is that *you can't be tense and relaxed at the same time.* When you feel tense, if you can relax your body, the tension will leave. It takes some practice, but after a while, you will learn the difference between what it feels like to be tense and what it feels like to be relaxed. When you feel yourself becoming tense, you can consciously relax your body.

These exercises involve first tensing each muscle group and then relaxing it. If you start to relax from a state of deliberately heightened tension, you build up a momentum so that the relaxation proceeds much further than it would if you started from a lower tension state. This also makes you aware of where and how you experience your tension. This awareness can serve as a signal for deliberate relaxation on your part when tension occurs. As we go through the major muscle groups in the body, you will tense each one, hold it for a count of five, and then relax it.

Practice these exercises in a quiet place where you can have some privacy. Find a comfortable bed or chair on which to relax. Turn off any bright lights and remove your glasses. Also, loosen any tight clothing or belt and remove your shoes.

When you're tensing a specific muscle group, try to keep the other muscles in your body relaxed. This isn't easy to do at first, but it will become easier with practice. When you tense a muscle group, don't tense it as tightly as you can, just tense it three-quarters of the way. When you relax that muscle group, just let it go and do nothing. Relaxation is doing nothing.

You may experience some unusual feelings like tingling or a floating sensation. These feelings are signs that your muscles are beginning to loosen. Or you may experience other feelings. You will remain in control of your body and can open your eyes and stop anytime you wish. Your mind may wander during the exercises, but don't worry about this. Just bring your thoughts back when you can. When you finish the exercises, you may stay where you are as long as you wish, but when you do get up, do it slowly, allowing the muscle tone to gradually come back.

Remember:

1. Being tense uses energy and can make you feel tired.
2. Try not to fall asleep while doing the exercises. They're great for insomnia, but we want your body to learn the difference between a tense muscle and a relaxed one. Your body isn't learning anything when you're sleeping.
3. You may say after a few times that you don't feel relaxed and that nothing is happening. But your body is learning many things, whether you are aware of it or not. Learning to relax is a skill, like learning to ride a bicycle, and takes time to learn.
4. Some people say that they feel out of control when they are relaxed. You may have that feeling at first, but actually you are gaining control of your body. Being able to relax your body when you feel anxious is taking control of it instead of letting it react in ways that increase your anxiety.
5. Do the exercise at least once a day for four weeks. It takes only twenty minutes, and it's better for your body than twenty minutes of sleep.

Anxiety rating scale

On a scale of one to ten, with one being completely relaxed and ten being extremely anxious, make a note of the number that best describes you before doing the relaxation exercises and again after you have completed them. Do this once a week for the next four weeks. It will help you to see the progress you are making in learning to relax.

TAPING THE RELAXATION EXERCISES   We suggest that you make a tape of the relaxation exercises or have a friend with a pleasant voice do it for you. Read the following script into the tape recorder in a soft, soothing voice. Read it slowly and allow seven to ten seconds between each paragraph. The entire exercise should take about twenty minutes. There is a description of a pleasant scene at the end of the exercises to help you relax your mind as well. If you like the scene and think that it is relaxing and pleasant, record it on your tape along with the exercises. If you have a personal favorite pleasant scene, use it instead. Use what will work for you.

Although you can easily make a tape of these exercises yourself, you may want to buy a prerecorded one. Listening to your own voice, or that of a friend, may be distracting as you try to relax. Also, a tape recorded by a person trained and experienced in relaxation therapy will have better pacing and voice quality. Information on where to purchase a relaxation tape is given at the end of this chapter.

RELAXATION SCRIPT   Settle back and relax as best as you can. Take a few deep breaths and begin to feel yourself let go.

Now, extend both arms straight in front of you, clenching your fists more and more tightly, and count, one . . . two . . . three . . . four . . . five. . . . Relax. Just let your arms drop wherever they will. Begin to appreciate the difference between the feelings of tension you felt a few seconds ago and now, the feelings of relaxation in your hands and arms.

Next, let's concentrate on the muscles in your forearms. Extend both arms straight out again, only this time push forward with your hands and count, one . . . two . . .

three . . . four . . . five. . . . Relax. Just let your arms go and concentrate on the warm feeling of relaxation flowing throughout your forearms.

Let's concentrate now on the muscles in your upper arms. To do this, bend both arms at the elbow and flex your biceps more and more and count, one . . . two . . . three . . . four . . . five. . . . Relax. Note the heavy, warm feelings associated with relaxation as they flow downward throughout your arms right to the tips of your fingers.

Let's concentrate now on the muscles in your forehead. Wrinkle up your forehead or frown by raising your eyebrows. One . . . two . . . three . . . four . . . five. . . . Relax. Let all the muscles in your forehead smooth out and become smoother and smoother.

Let's work on the area around your eyes and nose. Close your eyes more and more tightly and count, one . . . two . . . three . . . four . . . five. . . . Relax. While keeping your eyes closed, enjoy the soothing, calm feeling in your eyes.

Let's work on the area around your lips, cheeks, and jaw. Draw the corners of your mouth back farther; try to get that ear-to-ear grin. One . . . two . . . three . . . four . . . five. Relax. Just let your jaw hang loose. Appreciate the feeling of relaxation.

Now, grit your teeth and feel the tenseness in your throat muscles get greater and greater. Count to five. One . . . two . . . three . . . four . . . five. . . . Relax. Let your neck hang loose; let it relax at whatever position feels most comfortable. As you continue to relax further and further, your breathing becomes more and more regular.

Let's concentrate now on your shoulder muscles. Shrug your shoulders and try to touch them to your ears. One . . . two . . . three . . . four . . . five. . . . Relax. Let your shoulders slump and attend to the warm, tingling feelings as they flow throughout your shoulders and connect with the relaxation in your arms. Let the tingling feelings flow throughout your arms right to the tips of your fingers.

Let your whole body slump back into the chair. Let the chair support the weight of your body. Let your whole body relax further and further.

Now tighten your stomach muscles more and more and count. One . . . two . . . three . . . four . . . five. . . . Relax. Just let your stomach muscles go. Each time you breathe out, your stomach muscles relax. Each time you breathe in, this relaxation begins to flow throughout your entire body—further and further—you're breathing, freely and deeply, freely and deeply.

Shift your attention now to the muscles in your thighs. Straighten out both your legs and bend your toes back toward your head, feeling the tension in your thighs. One . . . two . . . three . . . four . . . five. . . . Relax. Let your legs drop and notice the difference in this area between the feelings of tension and now the feelings of relaxation. A warm, tingling feeling is flowing throughout your legs.

Straighten out both your legs again, but this time point your toes away from your head, tensing your calf muscles. One . . . two . . . three . . . four . . . five. . . . Relax.

No more tension at all now, nothing but relaxation. Enjoy the calm, soothing feeling of relaxation as it flows right to the tips of your toes. You're feeling very calm, very peaceful, very relaxed. To help you relax even further, let's mention the various muscle groups you've been tensing and relaxing, but this time don't tense them, simply relax them further and further. Try to get that extra bit of relaxation in each muscle group. Your forehead. The area around your eyes and nose. Your lips, cheeks, and jaw. Just begin to feel a wave of relaxation continue downward through your neck muscles, across your shoulder, down through your arms, right to the tips of your fingers. It's flowing across your chest, down your back, and into your stomach muscles.

Your breathing becomes more and more regular as the waves of relaxation continue downward through your thighs, into your calves, right to the tips of your toes. You're feeling very calm, very peaceful, very relaxed.

Imagine yourself outside, sitting in a soft, comfortable chair beside a small, rippling brook. It's a beautiful spring day. The sun is shining. The sky is blue with a few fluffy white clouds drifting by. The trees and grass are green, and a soft, warm breeze caresses your face now and then. It's very quiet and peaceful with just the faint chirping of birds in the background. You're feeling very calm, very peaceful, very relaxed.

The sun is shining through the leaves of the trees and glistens on the ripples of the brook. As you look upstream, you notice a leaf floating slowly downstream toward you. It rises and then falls on the gentle ripples of the water. Rises and falls. You continue to watch it as it drifts past you and floats slowly downstream until it's out of sight. You're feeling very calm, very peaceful, very relaxed.

PRERECORDED RELAXATION TAPES   For information on prerecorded relaxation tapes, write to: Carol Stauffer, Box 15410, Pittsburgh, PA 15237.

Passengers buy tickets and check baggage at the airline
counter. TV monitors above show arrival and departure times.
(USAir photo.)

Passengers relax in the airline waiting room before a flight.
(Photo by Dave Edwards, USAir.)

Behind the scenes, pilots converse with dispatcher by phone while planning a flight in the operations office. *(Photo by Jeff/Skip Budny.)*

Dispatchers aid the captain with the latest weather reports. Together they discuss whether a flight can be conducted safely. *(USAir photo.)*

A jet transport will emerge like new from a major overhaul.
(*USAir photo.*)

The captain checks the
control surface during a
walkaround inspection.
(*Photo by Jeff/Skip Budny.*)

The mechanic and pilot discuss tire conditions during inspection.
(Photo by Jeff/Skip Budny.)

Pilots set and check cockpit controls for departure.
(Photo by Jeff/Skip Budny.)

This cockpit looks like one in an actual aircraft, but the trainee and instructor are in a flight simulator. *(Photo by Jeff/Skip Budny.)*

Passengers board the plane through a jetway. *(Photo by Jeff/Skip Budny.)*

Comfortable seats beckon; there's space for carry-on luggage beneath. *(Photo by Jeff/Skip Budny.)*

Light, attendant call, and oxygen controls are overhead. *(Photo by Jeff/Skip Budny.)*

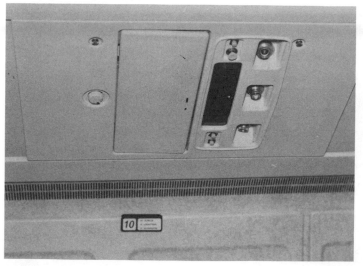

A flight attendant demonstrates the use of an oxygen mask and other emergency equipment. *(Photo by Jeff/Skip Budny.)*

Airport tower operators communicate with taxiing aircraft. *(Photo by Jeff/Skip Budny.)*

The control tower is more than one hundred feet high; the climbing jet will soon be thousands of feet high. *(Photo by Jeff/Skip Budny.)*

Traffic controllers in the radar room watch and communicate with the "blips" that represent the aircraft they are keeping separated in flight. *(Photo by Jeff/Skip Budny.)*

This airliner flies in clear skies above the clouds. *(USAir photo.)*

The plane has again landed, its flight safely and comfortably completed. *(USAir photo.)*

CHAPTER 6

The Safe Control
of Planes That Pass
in the Flight

TAKE, DON'T GIVE UP, CONTROL

Fearful flyers are reluctant to give control of their lives to an unseen crew in the front of the airplane—people they know nothing about. And then there are the flight attendants, mechanics, and air-traffic controllers to be concerned about. Most people don't even know that there are dispatchers involved and are only vaguely aware that government inspectors might have something to do with the control of the safety of their flight.

New knowledge about relaxation techniques will permit you to take over control of your own mind and body and to relax, even in situations that formerly felt out of your control. And knowledge about airplanes, how they fly, and how and by whom the flights are handled will permit you to fly more comfortably, assured that you are in good hands.

PILOTS

Pilots in the United States and in most of the western world usually begin flying for commercial airlines after logging thousands of flight hours and having attained years of experience in various other flying operations. These include the military services, commuter airlines, air taxis, charter services, and flight instruction. Although already well qualified in one or more of those fields, the pilot applying for employment with a commercial airline still has to prove him- or herself in a highly competitive hiring situation. There are generally many more available pilots than there are flight-crew jobs available. And of course the "proving" goes on throughout the pilot's flying career.

In some Third World and other countries, native pilots sometimes lack the opportunity to accumulate years and flying hours of experience. Concentrated and comprehensive training and checking make up for this, though, and they fly extensively as co-pilots for experienced captains until they are sufficiently qualified to assume command of an airliner. There is not a great deal of detail known about Russian and Eastern Bloc airline training, but it is generally acknowledged that those nations do place proper emphasis on the safety of their flights.

New pilots

A typical U.S. airline's hiring standard for a new pilot includes a Federal Aviation Administration (FAA) commercial license, which allows flying for hire; an instrument rating, which permits flying in nonvisual flight conditions (in clouds); and a multi-engine rating, with which the pilot can fly aircraft with more than one engine. Most airlines require that pilots have flown at least 2,000 hours, with a substantial portion of those hours in multi-engine flight and in actual bad-weather conditions. Most airlines today also require experience with turbine (jet) aircraft.

In these days of millions and billions, perhaps 2,000 flight hours doesn't sound like much. But anyone can learn to fly and be flying solo in a light trainer airplane after only about eight hours of instruction. So a pilot with 2,000 hours of flying time is truly experienced, at least in terms of hours flown.

Many airlines require that pilots hold a college degree or its equivalent, and all require that they be in excellent physical condition. Some airlines administer their own physical examinations, but all require that applicants pass an FAA First Class physical exam, administered by doctors trained and certified by the FAA. Various intelligence, aptitude, and psychological tests are administered in conjunction with personal interviews. Most carriers require that applicants pass an evaluation in either an airplane or a flight simulator. Pilots who favorably meet all these requirements are assigned to a training class.

New hires must then pass six to ten weeks of exacting training and testing before being assigned as regular flight-crew members.

Flight crews

Every airline flight has a crew consisting of at least a pilot and a co-pilot. Most airlines give the pilot the title of captain; the co-pilot is called the first officer. Many carriers operate aircraft that have a requirement for a third cockpit crew member, called a flight engineer or second officer. New hires may expect to be initially trained as either co-pilots or engineers.

Insignia and rank stripes vary with different carriers and countries, but typical captains wear four stripes on their sleeves and shoulder epaulets, and the cap visor contains an embroidered design (commonly called "scrambled eggs" by crew members). The first and second officers wear three stripes. Occasionally, a flight engineer may be spotted wearing only two stripes. This individual is either a career nonpilot engineer or perhaps a pilot who is over the age of sixty and is, under FAA regulations, no longer permitted to fly scheduled airliner flights as pilot.

The captain sits in the left front seat in the cockpit (sometimes called the flight deck). During the flight the captain is in command; he or she is responsible for the efficient conduct of the flight and for the safety of the aircraft, its passengers, its crew, and its cargo. (We'll see later that overall responsibility for the flight is shared by a flight dispatcher.)

The first officer occupies the right front seat and is second in command. Actual flying of the airliner is generally shared equally, subject to the captain's discretion. Duties during flight are allotted according to which "pilot is flying" and which "pilot is not flying."

The flight engineer, in aircraft that are configured to require one, occupies a seat behind the first officer, facing sideways or nearly so. This second officer faces a panel of gauges, lights, and switches that control most of the aircraft's systems—hydraulic, pressurization, heating and cooling, electrical, fuel, and the like. Some system controls are still retained on a central panel overhead. Even these are accessible to the second officer. On airplanes that don't require the third crew member, all system controls are located within easy reach of the pilots. Most new transport designs do not include engineer stations because today's largely automatic systems eliminate the need for a third person.

Qualification and advancement

The schooling that must be satisfactorily completed by new pilots at a major airline includes classroom study, hands-on practice on training devices, and in some instances training on interactive computer systems. There are hours of training, practice and testing in flight simulators, then training and testing in the actual aircraft. Cockpit observation flights of the regular crews at work round out the education of these recruits.

Fearful flyers, peering into the cockpit for the first time, often inquire, "Do the pilots have to know *all this?*" The answer is, "Yes, they do." New pilots learning about their assigned airplanes—or veteran pilots changing to a new-to-them type—must know the function of every control, the meaning of every light, the significance of every instrument indication. It's too bad that we don't learn as much about our automobiles as pilots must know about the planes they fly.

These new crew members can then be assigned to regular line flights as first or second officers. At most airlines, they are on probation for one year. Performance and behavior are closely monitored during this period.

The new pilots return to training and testing within their first year. This consists of recurrent ground schooling and a proficiency training session in a flight simulator.* All pilots are scheduled for the refresher classroom training every twelve months. Also, they receive proficiency training

* The actual aircraft is used for proficiency checks at carriers where simulators are not available.

alternately with proficiency checks—captains every six months, the others every year. Captains receive at least one route check each year administered by an FAA-designated company check pilot and possibly another by an FAA inspector. All training and checking must be satisfactorily completed before pilots, new or experienced, can return to flight duties.

Consistent with their seniority and available job openings, pilots are free to bid on flying different types of aircraft. Also, they can advance to different crew positions. For instance, a captain flying an older-type Boeing 727 aircraft could choose to fly a new 767. But to do this he or she would have to undergo ground, simulator, and aircraft training as necessary to make the transition to that aircraft. It takes from six to ten weeks to complete this training.

A flight engineer can advance to a co-pilot position; a co-pilot can advance to a pilot position. The training given for this type of move is termed upgrading. Again, six to ten weeks of training is required for this type of move.

In addition to these continuous qualification requirements, crews receive information bulletins, manual revisions, and any special training as needed. Crews feel as though they're perpetually going to school. There is probably no profession that subjects its members to such ongoing proficiency testing. That proficiency is maintained at the highest level by this rigorous system of checks and balances, cross-checks, and standardization.

A Thought to Fly by

If you have to relinquish a measure of control to others, you couldn't pick a better group than airline pilots.

FLIGHT DISPATCHERS

We mentioned earlier that the captain is responsible for the flight, both by government regulation and by company policy. Airlines that operate large aircraft on regularly scheduled flights also employ dispatchers who share that responsibility. They're part of a flight control or system control function; no flight can operate unless the captain and the dispatcher agree that each aspect of the flight can be conducted safely. Either can cancel an entire flight or a portion of it.

In the aircraft cockpit the captain receives all the weather and airport condition information needed to ensure that the planned flight can be operated according to these priorities: safety, passenger comfort and convenience, and schedule.

Flight dispatchers have a somewhat bigger picture before them than does the flight crew as they jointly plan a flight operation. The dispatch office is normally located at an airline headquarters facility, handy to aircraft routing and crew scheduling functions. There are direct communication lines to airport stations, weather services, maintenance facilities, airport control towers, and FAA airway traffic control centers.

The flight dispatcher observes the same priorities as the flight crew, but the dispatcher's planning also considers economic aspects of the operation, its place in the overall scheme of company flights, and the effect of decisions on service to passengers and cargo customers. International flights become more involved with trans-border operations and regulations. Captains are responsible only for *their* flights; dispatchers have a number of flights assigned to them.

To initiate operation of a flight, the dispatcher issues a flight release to the captain at the originating station. A typical release specifies the flight number; the originating, en route, and terminating airports scheduled for landing; whether the flight is authorized to operate under Instrument or Visual Flight Rules (IFR/VFR); alternate airport(s); minimum fuel needed at each fueling point; flight plan information; and any other data the dispatcher desires to pass along to the captain. The dispatcher concludes the flight release with the release time, his or her name, and his or her telephone number.

The captain may desire changes to the release. He or she could request more fuel or less fuel, a change in or an addition to the alternate airport(s), and so on. If the changes are satisfactory to the dispatcher after consultation, the release is revised.

A Thought to Fly by

The captain and the dispatcher *must agree* that each phase of the flight can be conducted safely.

As the flight leaves the originating station and proceeds through any intermediate stops to the final destination, the dispatcher "follows" it, monitoring its progress to provide the captain with continuing information required for the flight's safe completion. He or she anticipates and watches weather and other current condition changes that might affect the flight. The dispatcher and the captain can communicate at any time during the flight. They operate as a team.

The dispatchers may or may not be pilots themselves. Often they are medically retired pilots. But pilots or not, they are knowledgeable about all phases of flight operation. The FAA's written and practical examinations, which they must pass to obtain their dispatcher certificates, rival those required of pilots when they upgrade to captain.

Dispatchers at established airlines often come up through the ranks of agents experienced in station operation. There they become familiar with all aspects of airline operation—weather, airport conditions, air-traffic control, communications, delayed or other irregular operations, and interacting with airport authorities, FAA facilities and personnel, and other airline departments. Beginning with dispatch clerk, advancement to dispatcher status can take many years.

FLIGHT ATTENDANTS

At least flight attendants seem real—unlike the pilots, they can be seen. Some people say they always keep their eyes on those faces. If they look worried during the flght, these passengers reason, then fear is justified. But any concerned expression probably means only that a coffee maker just went on the blink, her feet hurt, or he had a parting argument with his wife that morning.

Much of the training for the women and men who control an airliner's passenger cabin is mandated by FAA regulation; the airlines then add their own concerns and their own emphasis on particular areas. A typical airline program for new-hire attendants encompasses six weeks of classroom participation and on-the-job training on numerous scheduled flights. Training days are of eight to twelve hours in duration. Much individual study is required to achieve the high test scores required by the airline. Typically, 90 percent is considered passing.

The school's curriculum contains numerous subjects tuned to the customer service aspect of flight attendant (F/A) duties. A partial list: airline routes and city codes, cabin announcements and demonstrations, food and beverage service, personal appearance and voice diction, and care of disabled passengers and unaccompanied children.

F/A instruction that should reassure fearful flyers includes aircraft familiarization, cabin-safety rules, emergency equipment location and use, aircraft emergency exits and evacuation, first aid and medical emergencies, emergency responsibilities and procedures, security measures, and irregular operations, such as planes diverted to alternate airports, flight cancellations, mechanical difficulties, and so forth.

The intensive qualification program also contains study on the theory of flight, federal aviation regulations, flight attendant work and conduct rules, and company policies and procedures. For overseas airlines there are international procedures and regulations to be learned.

Emergency drills (location and use of emergency equipment; cabin evacuation, including practice in opening emergency exits and in deploying and using evacuation slides; and use of fire extinguishers) are conducted either on full-size mockups or on actual aircraft. F/As actually put out fires with the various types of extinguishers aboard, open emergency exits, and jump onto inflated evacuation slides. If their airline flies over water, they practice with life preservers and inflatable seat cushions. Where life rafts are installed they get wet in actual water drills in which they deploy and board the rafts.

Cabin service instruction and practice takes place first in cabin mockups or in aircraft on the ground. During actual flights, the new attendants conduct cabin service under the watchful eyes of the regular crew. After graduation from the initial training course, the men and women are assigned to flights.

Every twelve months, flight attendants attend one- or two-day recurrent classes. This refresher training maintains proficiency levels and provides the attendants with new or revised information. At least once every twenty-four months, the emergency drills are again practiced. This phase of retraining is necessary because very little of an emergency nature ever occurs on regular flights. Remember that 99-plus percent of all scheduled flights are normal. Very few flight attendants will actually encounter an emergency situation during their careers. But they're ready for it, thanks to their initial and continuing training.

Supervisory personnel periodically conduct checks on each individual, observing to ensure that proper procedures are followed. Attendants throughout the year receive manual revisions and bulletins on changes in or additions to policies, procedures, and regulations. All this, and personal motivation for their own safety and comfort, keep flight attendants prepared for all their passengers, fearful or fearless.

OPERATIONS AGENTS

The role of the airline operations agent on the ground encompasses the following responsibilities:

- Obtaining and communicating current weather conditions and forecasts at that city station, also at other required or requested points.

- Reporting on field conditions. In winter, especially, current information on snow or ice coverage of runways, taxiways, and ramps is important.
- Controlling the loading of passengers, baggage, and cargo to ensure that the plane departing the station meets rigid weight and balance requirements. Ten pounds overweight is as illegal as 1,000 pounds overweight.
- Sometimes relaying pilot requests for air-traffic control clearances and then transmitting ATC's clearance to the captain (this is done most often at smaller airports without control towers or other FAA facilities).
- Performing as the liaison between the flight's dispatcher and its captain en route to and from the agent's station.

MECHANICS

The stereotypical view of an aircraft mechanic is of a greasy guy in baggy overalls with his hat on backward and an oil-soaked rag and a wrench sticking out of a back pocket. Some mechanics today certainly can still go home with hydraulic-fluid stains on their shoes and grease spots on their parkas. But mechanics also work in shopcoats in spotless "clean rooms" on sophisticated instruments. Or they sit at computers, analyzing the health of a particular engine that might be still in flight, 1,000 miles away.

Maintenance personnel may still be general practitioners, like country doctors. But many are specialists, graduated from fixing everything from wheels to wings, to trouble-shooting and then fine tuning an engine fuel control unit. Most of the line maintenance people are the first type and are prepared to satisfy any logbook complaint of the flight crew that flew the plane in. The majority of these logbook writeups are taken care of by replacement of the faulty unit. The faulty unit is then sent to the airline maintenance shops for a simple fix or a complete overhaul by the specialists or by the unit's manufacturer. The newly installed unit has to test properly before the mechanic "writes off" the complaint, allowing the plane to resume its travels.

Mechanics' training and licensing

Ninety percent of the maintenance personnel of today's typical airline are licensed by the FAA. The basic rating is an Airframe and Powerplant (A&P) certificate. It is earned by the satisfactory completion of written and practical examinations after at least two years of study and on-the-job practice. Most mechanics train with aviation trade schools or with military aviation forces. Those who will specialize in electronics and avionics require a radio rating rather than the A&P. Between graduating from the trade school and hiring on with a larger scheduled airline, most mechanics serve apprenticeships with commuter airlines, cargo or charter lines, or flight training schools (including colleges).

Airline qualification training for the newly hired mechanics is conducted for a number of weeks. This training consists of classroom and hands-on sessions. They receive familiarization training on the systems, powerplants, and servicing equipments of each aircraft type. Where individuals are to be assigned specialized tasks, they receive specialized training. On-the-job training is both necessary and effective; it's conducted by more experienced mechanics, by instructors, or by lead mechanics or foremen.

Airline mechanics routinely receive training bulletins on many subjects: on avionics, on flight controls, on hydraulics and pneumatics, even on aircraft cleaning. This last is important to airlines not only because it assures passengers that the plane is well cared for, but also to ward off corrosion, or to prevent foreign material from entering sophisticated components.

Mechanics are regularly assigned to recurrent training classes. This is both as a refresher on previously learned skills and also to learn new or revised procedures or to become acquainted with new equipment.

Airline mechanics are highly trained, skilled, and motivated to present a well-maintained airplane for the crews and the customers to fly in. They have control over whether an airplane is considered ready to fly or not. It must be airworthy, or the mechanic will not sign his or her name on the aircraft maintenance log. Even beyond this, however, the airline's own inspectors (they report to an independent inspection department rather than to maintenance) and the FAA's inspectors are continually monitoring the maintenance process. It's an effective system of checks and balances.

GOVERNMENT SURVEILLANCE: FAA'S SAFETY INSPECTORS

FAA safety inspectors cover the two main functions of operations and maintenance. Inspectors for general (private) aviation combine these functions somewhat while inspectors of the air carriers are more specialized. FAA pilot specialists oversee flight operations for the airlines while FAA mechanic specialists watch over airline maintenance and engineering.

These government inspectors work with airline management in the development, approval, and monitoring of airline programs, including training, operations, and maintenance. Operations inspectors are in contact with the flight crews as they conduct surveillance on ground school classes, simulator and aircraft training sessions, and scheduled flight operations (including charter flights). They appear, unannounced, to occupy an observation seat in the cockpit of a flight. They evaluate all aspects of cockpit and cabin crew performance. Maintenance inspectors conduct similar surveillance in the shops and hangars and on the ramps.

Inspectors join the FAA after accumulating experience with the military services, airlines, or general aviation. They attend formal training programs at the FAA Academy at Oklahoma City. In addition to weeks of intensive classroom and workshop training, the new inspectors undergo training in practical application of the surveillance function.

AIR-TRAFFIC CONTROL

The admittedly crowded skies of the United States are safe for air travelers. If they weren't, your flight's captain would not have you up there. He would not be up there himself.

Today, however, the public perceives that the FAA's Air Traffic Control (ATC) system is not a safe one. The numerous media recountings of near-misses, controller errors, pilots landing on wrong runways or even wrong airports presents an unnerving picture for the traveler—especially for nervous passengers like you.

But if you read the smaller print, if you listen to the quieter words summing up the situation, most will tell you that the system is safe, but it can be made safer. The U.S. Air Traffic Control System accommodates more than 17,000 airline flights each day, but it must be expanded and improved to safely accommodate a doubling of that number before the year 2000.

ATC will never knowingly put airplanes into the air in an unsafe situation. Controllers must observe the airspace limitations that keep aircraft separated. Put simply, planes are kept five miles apart when under ATC Center control, and three miles apart when under airport tower control. Flights are also separated vertically, by at least 1,000 feet, 2,000 at the highest altitudes. Flights are not permitted into airspace where there would be conflict—instead, they are held on the ground or held in the air a safe distance from the other traffic. We're talking mostly about delay, not danger.

A Thought to Fly by

When there are more flights than airspace, it means delay, not danger.

The U.S. ATC system, which recently celebrated its fiftieth year of operation, is the largest and best in the world; it forms the basis for similar systems worldwide. ATC provides nationwide traffic control from the departure ramp to arrival at the destination gate.

Airplanes fly by one of two sets of FAA rules—Visual Flight Rules (VFR) or Instrument Flight Rules (IFR). Airlines fly almost exclusively IFR. General aviation planes can fly IFR if their planes are properly equipped and their pilots are qualified for instrument flight. Flying VFR, pilots may come into contact only with airport traffic control towers. Even they are not available at small airports, and pilots provide their own visual separation from one another, a process that is generally augmented by radio communication.

Airport traffic-control tower

As many as one hundred aircraft per hour take off or land at busy airports every day. Responsibility for the safe, orderly flow of these takeoffs and landings belongs to the air traffic controllers in the FAA's more than 400 airport control towers, located at the nation's busiest airports.

In a typical large airline operation, flight plans for every scheduled flight are filed into FAA computers one month in advance. Captains are free to revise the flight plan for a particular trip they are to fly. Thus, they may request a higher or lower altitude to minimize turbulence or a different routing to avoid thunderstorms or icing conditions.

Except for certain high-density airports where a reservation system is used (such as John F. Kennedy, Newark International, and La Guardia Airports in the New York area, Washington National Airport, and Chicago's O'Hare), arrival or departure at a tower-controlled airport is on a first-come, first-served basis, regardless of the size of the aircraft or the number of persons on board.

At all FAA tower-equipped airports, use of the runways is directed by a local controller in the glass-walled tower cab, which often adjoins the main terminal building. Aircraft are allowed to take off or land in much the same manner as surface traffic is moved through a busy intersection by a policeman, but in place of hand signals, radio communication is used to sequence aircraft movements. The controller also provides the pilot with certain essential flight information—principally the runway in active use, wind direction and velocity, and altimeter setting (barometric pressure). On the ground, aircraft are directed to and from parking areas by radio contact with a ground controller.

Towers normally control traffic in a thirty-mile radius of an airport.

Air route traffic-control centers

The tower controller transfers control of departing IFR aircraft to the nearest air route radar traffic control center. Under radar surveillance and in frequent radio contact, IFR aircraft are assigned a particular flight level and air route, are passed along from one center to the adjoining one (20 centers are located about 200 miles apart throughout the contiguous United States), and are finally turned over to the tower controller at the arrival airport.

The center controller depends on radar to see traffic. (The ATC system can still operate safely without radar but at a slower pace, and this invites flight delays.) Banks of radar scopes reveal the progress of all aircraft within a 200-mile radius. The aircraft, blips of light on the scope, are identified through voice contact or automatically (when the aircraft is equipped with a radar-responding device called a transponder). A data tag includes an altitude reading and plane speed.

Flight service stations

All aircraft, including airliners, may make use of FAA flight service stations (these are known as FSS), although these facilities primarily service general aviation pilots—whose number exceeds 700,000 in the United States. Located at airports, the flight service station is essentially a communications center with a radio range extending from 100 to 200 miles. (Many flight service stations are being combined and automated; the new facilities extend radio communication range over a considerable distance.) Specialists at the station provide pre-flight and in-flight briefings that include pertinent information about weather, airports, altitudes, routes, and other flight-planning data.

How controllers are qualified

Air-traffic control specialists work in the three areas of towers, centers, and flight service stations. Much of their training is the same for all of these, but there are specialized requirements, depending on the area to which they are assigned.

To qualify for one of the positions, an applicant must pass a comprehensive written test with a score of 85 or above and must have three years of general experience (administrative, technical, progressively responsible work) or four years of college, or any combination of education and experience equaling three years. Maximum entry age is thirty-one. Applicants must maintain a current FAA first-class medical certificate. This is the same physical standard that an airline captain must meet. Many newly hired controllers have piloting experience or traffic control experience with the military.

Following initial screening, trainees undergo sixteen weeks of training at the FAA Academy in Oklahoma City. The academy uses sophisticated computer systems to simulate the airport and airway environments in which the controllers will operate. They fully understand the ATC system when they leave the Academy and then put it into practice in the actual environment of their duty station. FAA Academy training is followed by extensive on-the-job training in specialized tasks. It takes years to completely qualify as a full duty controller.

In summation, we may say that many more highly qualified persons than just the pilots are ensuring safe control of the flight of your airliner from departure to destination.

CHAPTER 7

Snap!
Stop That Thought

Relaxation exercises will help your body feel comfortable and relaxed on an airplane, and thought-stopping techniques will free your mind of all those frightening and scary thoughts that you now have about flying.

"Thought stopping" means stopping a fearful thought every time it occurs and replacing it with a contradictory thought or a pleasant thought of any kind. It's a proven cognitive therapy to change obsessive or anxiety-evoking thinking. Our thoughts precede our emotions, so if you are constantly thinking fearful thoughts, you are going to feel anxious and experience those uncomfortable and scary physical symptoms we discussed earlier. You may have heart palpitations, sweating, nausea, trembling, cold hands or feet, shortness of breath, or muscle tension. If you can stop the fearful thoughts, you will stop the fearful feelings.

It is possible to take control of your thoughts (all of you control people should like this) and choose what you think about. This in turn will lower your anxiety or make it go away entirely. Your mind is a wonderful thing, but it can think of only one thing at a time! It can flit back and forth between two thoughts, but it can hold only one thought at a time.

At present, when someone mentions flying to you, it sets off all sorts of fearful thoughts in your mind. You may keep going over one fearful thought, or you may begin thinking about one thing, which then leads to a worse thought, which leads to a worse one and so on and so on. One fearful flyer kept a scrapbook filled with newspaper clippings about every negative thing he had ever read about airplanes and flying. He periodically paged through the book, re-reading each article. By doing this, he was reinforcing his fear of flying. Your fearful thoughts are doing the same thing.

A Thought to Fly by

Fearful thoughts are serving no useful purpose whatsoever and help only to maintain your fear.

HOW FEARFUL THOUGHTS ARE MAINTAINED

Most fearful flyers don't need a scrapbook to remind them of all the negative things they have ever heard or read about flying. They have them filed away somewhere in their memory bank to pull out when needed. They use them to justify their fears when confronted with the idea of flying; they can say, "See, I told you it was unsafe! I'm not getting on that plane!" They never pay attention to the *positive* side of flying.

Granted, the positive side is almost never presented in the media. Think about the last time you saw a headline reading NO AIRLINE ACCIDENTS IN 18 MONTHS! or OVER 17,000 AIRLINERS TAKE OFF AND LAND EACH DAY IN THE UNITED STATES WITHOUT A SINGLE ACCIDENT! You never did, of course, because it isn't newsworthy.

Not only do you read for weeks about airline accidents when they do occur, but you also constantly read about airline accidents that might have occurred. Reports of near-misses are in the newspapers all the time. The near-miss may have been when a plane strayed one mile out of the five-mile separation requirement between planes. Fearful flyers don't know that this is what happened and just remember the words *near-miss* and think that the two planes nearly collided, even though they were still four miles apart.

This doesn't mean that there are never instances when two planes are closer together than they should be. Human error does happen, but when you hear reports of the number of near-misses per year and that the number is rising, remember that the figure also includes planes that were not dangerously close but had just strayed a short distance out of the legal separation.

Interestingly enough, the media don't report near-misses in other forms of transportation. Have you ever heard a news report saying that two buses came within a few feet of each other on the interstate? Of course not, but it happens all the time.

Since we are deluged with negative information about flying, fearful flyers need to learn about the other side—the side we are presenting in this book. You need to give equal time to the positive side of flying. We think it deserves more than equal time since flying is such a safe way to travel, but we'll be satisfied if you at least give it equal time. We're not asking you to deny your fear or push it under the rug, but we are asking you to consider the new information and become an informed and educated flyer.

New Thoughts

You can think of only one thing at a time.
You can choose what you think about.
Fearful thoughts maintain your fear.
Fearful thoughts make you feel tense and anxious.
If the thoughts can be controlled, you will be more comfortable and relaxed.

WAYS TO USE THOUGHT STOPPING

Most of you use thought-stopping methods every day. If you have teenagers old enough to drive, you've probably lain awake at night worrying about them. If they're late getting home, all kinds of thoughts go through your mind: They've run out of gas, had a flat tire on a lonely road, or, even worse, been in a terrible accident. You think of every terrible thing that could possibly happen and end up unable to sleep until they get home.

If this goes on for too many nights, you begin to realize that you'll have to either stop thinking about all of these things or lock your kids in their rooms each night. You finally start to fill your mind with more positive and realistic thoughts. You tell yourself that he or she is fine, that no news is good news, and so on. You are using thought stopping in an unstructured, unsystematic way, but you are using it.

Thought stopping is often used as an adjunct to other types of psychotherapy. It works especially well with depressed clients. Depressed people often think that they are failures and keep going over and over all the negative things they have ever done or all the bad things that have ever happened to them—they never give equal time to the positive things. Going over these mistakes serves no purpose, makes them more depressed, and keeps them from taking any positive action. Some of them have thought this way for so long that they don't know how to break these thought patterns. Thought-stopping techniques help them to do this.

Thought stopping has also been used effectively with people in hospitals. Patients often become anxious before surgery. They have to sign beforehand a consent form that lists all the things that could possibly go wrong. They then begin to concentrate on these things and become even more anxious. Their blood pressure may rise; they often become nauseated, get headaches, or, at the very least, are unable to sleep. This is exactly the opposite from the condition the doctor would like them to be in before surgery! Thought stopping helps them to relax and concentrate on the positive aspects of their surgery or to think about some other positive or pleasant thing in their lives.

These people are taught to apply the thought-stopping techniques in a systematic and structured way, and the techniques reduce or eliminate their anxiety. These same methods can help you to eliminate your fear of flying. You may think that although you can stop fearful thoughts for a few seconds, they will come right back. At first they will, but with practice, they'll occur less and less frequently and eventually cease to be a problem.

STOPPING THOSE FEARFUL THOUGHTS

Every time you have a fearful or negative thought about flying, say "stop" in a loud voice and *stop* thinking that thought. This is easy to do if you are alone, but if you are with other people you may not, for obvious reasons, want to say "stop" aloud. In that case, put a rubber band on your wrist and wear it for the next month. Every time you have a fearful thought about flying, imagine yourself saying "stop" and gently flick the rubber band. After a while, just looking at the rubber band will remind you to stop the fearful thoughts. You must be consistent. You must stop every single fearful or negative thought about flying. Even if it isn't a specific frightening thought, but just a generalized anxiety about flying, *stop* it.

After one week of practicing stopping the fearful thoughts, start to replace them with a contradictory thought or a pleasant thought of any kind. You just can't leave a void in your mind after you have stopped the fearful thought. If you don't put a new thought into that void, the fearful thought will surely come back.

A contradictory thought is one that negates your old fearful worry by providing you with new information about flying. If you were concerned about turbulence, some good thought replacers or stoppers could be: "turbulence won't hurt you or the airplane if you're in your seat with your seat belt fastened"; "the plane is flying in an ocean of air"; "turbulence is similar to the waves in the water or the bumps on a country road." Another replacer is that "planes do not come apart in turbulence, and the pilot does not lose control of the plane."

Here are some more thought stoppers:

- Planes can fly with only one engine.
- Planes just don't fall out of the sky—they can glide.
- Pilots want to reach their destination safely as much as you do.
- Increase in the number of planes flying makes for more delays, not for less safety.

The aviation education in this book should provide you with stoppers to all of your old fearful thoughts.

But what if your fear isn't about the plane or the pilots, but about how you will react when they close that door and you can't get off? If you're claustrophobic, afraid of heights, or afraid of not having control, you may wonder how thought stopping can help.

What you are really afraid of are those awful symptoms you get when you become anxious. If you can break into that anxiety cycle when it first begins, it will never get to the point where you feel overwhelmed, out of control, or panicky. Thought stopping will help you keep anxiety at a very low level or make it disappear completely.

You may still consider yourself claustrophobic, afraid of heights, or afraid of not having control, but if you're sitting in that airplane seat, feeling comfortable and relaxed, it won't matter at all.

Here are some thought stoppers that will help control anxiety:

- I can't be tense and relaxed at the same time.
- If I know how to relax my body, I can do it even in fearful situations.
- I can't be panicky and relaxed at the same time.
- If I practice the relaxation exercises, I can relax my body even on an airplane.

- Relaxation and thought stopping do stop anxiety.
- Thousands have overcome their fear of flying using relaxation and thought stopping.
- Even if I am claustrophobic, fearful of heights, or fearful of not having control, I can learn to relax my body and mind and fly comfortably.

After you have finished reading this book, think about the things that were reassuring to you and that contradict your fears. Write four of them on a note card. You can use any of the examples we have given if they were meaningful to you. If you can't come up with a specific thought that helps, you can write down a pleasant thought of any kind. *The idea is to stop the fearful thought and replace it.* This will break up the anxiety and reduce it or make it go away entirely. We would like you to replace it with some new information, but the important thing is to stop it and replace it.

Here are some pleasant thought stoppers:

- A vacation spot.
- Sitting on my back porch on a summer night.
- A favorite person.
- A fantasy.

Carry your note card with you in your purse or pocket. Keep a copy on your desk or at a spot near you during the day. Have these new thoughts at your fingertips so that you can have them instantly available when you need them. You will be amazed at how well thought stopping works to alleviate those old fearful thoughts. It takes some practice, so don't get discouraged. Just keep doing it, and you will see results. Start to do it for other worries or concerns that you have. Think about your problems, try to solve them, and then use thought stopping to keep these problems from taking over your thoughts. But we want you to use it consistently and systematically for the fear of flying.

SUMMARY

Every time you have a fearful or negative thought about flying,

1. If you're alone, say aloud, "Stop!"
2. If you're with other people, imagine yourself saying "stop" or snap a rubber band on your wrist.
3. Replace the fearful thought with a contradictory thought or a pleasant thought of any kind.
4. On a note card, write four reassuring things that you have learned about flying and one pleasant thought.
5. Be consistent. Stop every fearful thought and replace it.

It takes practice, but fearful thoughts will occur less and less frequently and will eventually cease to be a problem.

A FOUR-WEEK DESENSITIZATION PLAN

Now that you've read about progressive relaxation and thought stopping, it's time to practice these methods in a systematic and structured way. People sometimes practice them for a few days, decide they don't work, and stop doing them. You can't teach your body and mind new behaviors in just a few days. You must practice the methods consistently for at least four weeks before they will be effective. The following plan gives you step-by-step instructions to do this.

As your body and mind learn to relax, you should then begin to gradually pair up this relaxed feeling with airports and airplanes. This is called systematic desensitization and entails gradually approaching the feared object or situation. The more times you pair up a relaxed feeling with an airplane (even if you're just watching that plane), the more comfortable you will be on an actual flight.

The four-week plan suggests making trips to the airport, watching planes, and, if possible, sitting on an airplane. The first time you go to the airport, you may feel some anxiety, but it will lessen each time you do this—providing you are practicing the relaxation and thought stopping.

Week 1

- Buy a small cassette player with earphones.
- Make a relaxation tape from the outline given in Chapter 5.
- Practice the exercises (using the tape) at least once a day.

Week 2

- Continue to practice with the relaxation tape at least once a day.
- Begin to do the thought-stopping procedures.
- Take a trip to the airport. Sit in your car in the parking lot or in a spot where you can see the airplanes landing and taking off. Do the relaxation exercises. Watch the planes for one half hour.

Week 3

- Continue to do the relaxation exercises every day.
- Use the thought-stopping methods consistently, write down your thought stoppers on a note card, and carry it with you.
- Go into the airport and have lunch or browse in the gift shop.
- Find a place to sit and listen to your relaxation exercises. You don't have to do them, just put the earplug in and listen.
- If there are windows or an observation deck, watch the planes for fifteen minutes.
- Go outside the terminal and watch the planes take off and land for fifteen minutes.

Week 4

- Do the relaxation exercises once a day.
- Use the thought stopping.
- Call the airport and ask which airline has the most flights per day. Call that airline and ask to speak to the customer service manager. Ask if there is a time when it is possible to go into an airplane and sit for a few minutes. (If this person is not helpful, say that you will call another airline to see if they can help you. Remember, airlines want your business and will try to be helpful.)
- Go to the airport. Go inside, find a seat, and listen to the relaxation exercises.
- Walk to the ticket counter and observe.
- Go to the security area and observe.
- If you are allowed to go through security, go to the gate area and sit for fifteen minutes.
- If you have made arrangements to sit on a plane, do so, and if there is time, do the relaxation exercises on the plane. (You are pairing up a relaxed feeling with an airplane.)
- Do all of the preceding in a relaxed, leisurely fashion.

CHAPTER 8

The Care and Feeding
of the Flying Machines

MISCONCEPTIONS

In the last twenty-five or so years, only 2 percent of airline accidents have been caused by maintenance problems. This is probably surprising to many fearful flyers. We know from talking with hundreds of you that you think that:

- Airplanes are not built strong enough to begin with.
- They weaken with use and with age.
- Airline maintenance has suffered under deregulation.
- Airlines cut corners to cut costs and service delays.
- Airlines keep older, worn-out planes in service.
- Mechanics are poorly trained and careless, and they try to convince pilots that the planes are okay mechanically.
- Overall, airlines are spending less for maintenance today than they did a few years ago.

These are misconceptions, and we'll reassure you about them.

STRUCTURAL FAILURES

In earlier years, after World War II, airliners were often plagued with mechanical problems: engine failures, leaking hydraulics and fuel lines, nonfunctioning heaters and de-icers, and radio and other electrical malfunctions. Today, airplanes are being built stronger (although lighter); their engines, systems, and components have become extremely dependable; and their maintenance has been made surer and easier because of swift advances in technology. Me-chanics still probe airplane innards through access panels as they have for fifty years, but maintenance also uses X rays, sonic waves, and computers to gauge the health of the aircraft and to prescribe for any illness. Accidents due to faulty maintenance or to actual failure of any airplane part or component are extremely rare—they're largely part of the dim past.

But what about the structural failures found in an airliner and in engines in 1985? That's not the "dim past."

True. But, again, accidents from such failures are extremely rare. A Japanese 747 crashed in 1985 when the pilots could no longer control the big airplane (as they had for many minutes) because some of their tail surfaces had been, in effect, blown away. This was caused by the rear pressure bulkhead rupturing, allowing pressurized air from the cabin to rush through the openings with a force that took some of the plane's control surfaces with it.

The reason for the rupture dated back seven years when the flight crew reported a hard landing. The hard-landing inspection revealed that internal body damage had been done. That rear bulkhead, the rearmost cap of the pressurized container that is the passenger cabin, had a split in it. A team from the builder of the 747 repaired the bulkhead, and the plane flew for seven more years until the accident. The investigation then revealed that the repair was flawed. The important thing about this accident is that it was one of a very few structural failures that have occurred in flight.

A couple of years earlier, a DC-10 accident occurred in Chicago during a takeoff. An engine broke loose from its mounting on the wing and flipped over the top of the wing. This alone would not have had to be catastrophic —no more so than any engine failure on takeoff, which is safely and surely handled by the crew. But in this particular instance, the loosened engine damaged fluid control lines in the wing, and the pilots were unable to continue controlling the aircraft.

The reason for the engine mount's failure was traced to a maintenance procedure that the airline had recently adopted. When this particular engine was re-installed after routine maintenance on the plane, part of the mounting structure cracked, undetected. After many flights, during this takeoff the mount broke completely. The maintenance procedure, of course, was quickly reverted back to the one that the manufacturer recommended. (It should be noted that airlines have the right—even the responsibility—to modify manufacturers' procedures based on their learned experience operating the airplane every day. They then take responsibility for the change. Often, manufacturers then change *their* recommended procedures based on airline experience.)

From this DC–10 incident, in addition to focusing

worldwide attention on that particular maintenance procedure, the following changes resulted:

- Protection of DC–10 vital hydraulic units and plumbing was increased as necessary, along with other control mechanisms and cables.
- Other types of aircraft were analyzed to ensure that similar situations would not be encountered with them.
- Pilots' flight procedures were modified where necessary to ensure that sufficient airspeed would be maintained to provide in-flight control of the airplane with a problem such as this.

Searching for structural-failure accidents before these two relatively recent ones, we have to go back to 1953–54 to the first turbojet transports, the British Comets, which developed cracks in the fuselage below the cabin windows. Also back in the 1950s, Lockheed Electra jet prop transports experienced wing structural failures in air turbulence. Both of these airliners were taken out of service, the design flaws were corrected, and the aircraft were put back into use, perfectly safe. With the exception of such isolated examples, structural failure causing serious accidents has been, and is, an extremely rare occurrence with airliners.

Look back again to 1985. With the startling figure of nearly 2,000 airline deaths that occurred worldwide that year, safety experts look for a pattern or some common thread that could explain what had happened.* This was not found in 1985. Every accident was different; the two that came closest to a common thread were both caused by engine failure. But accidents due to jet engine failure are still extremely rare. As discussed in Chapter 2, jet engines are

---

*There were 196 fatalities in U.S. scheduled airline flights. A U.S. military charter crash in Newfoundland caused 233 deaths.

amazingly dependable and are becoming increasingly so. This is true also for propjet engines, and it should also be true for the jet engines that drive new-design prop fans that are coming on line in the 1990s.

AGE OF AIRLINERS

Aircraft and engines and the numerous other units that make up the modern airplane are designed to be rugged, to operate for many hours before replacement or even repair. Even so, important parts and systems are checked and changed often enough that the plane doesn't really grow old.

DC-3s, the airliners that formed the basis of the airline networks of the whole world, first flew in service in 1935. There are still 2,000 of them flying routes in numerous countries. Two *Air Force One* airplanes, which fly the president and vice president of the United States around the world, were recently replaced by new models after more than twenty years of continuous service. Modernizing modifications and proper maintenance programs keep these birds young and flying for as long as their operators want them to remain in service.

Although maintenance costs do rise somewhat with the aging process, it is not normally the age of the airplanes that cause airline management to replace them. Rather, it is the size and/or the efficient performance (flying more payload at greater speeds and less cost) of the planes that triggers fleet renewal. Newer aircraft and engines are designed to be quieter and more fuel efficient, and to fly longer before major maintenance is required.

THOSE BEAUTIFUL FLYING MACHINES

All of you may not agree that airliners are beautiful. We know that many fear them, so they may also loathe them, may even think they're ugly. Pilots think all airplanes—trainers, transports, fighters, bombers—are beautiful. And they want you to love them, and love flying, also.

Beauty is only skin deep, but the "skin" of airliners is quite thick. And there's an extremely strong bone structure beneath. We've allowed thousands of fearful flyers to pound on the fuselage and on the wings (along with kicking the tires), and every one has been impressed by the rigidity and the obvious strength. Airplanes are built as light as possible, but strength isn't sacrificed to keep the weight down.

New metal alloys and composite structures currently make planes lighter yet stronger. This goes for interiors as well as exteriors, and everything in between. Also, the interiors have increasingly become more attractive and more utilitarian.

Most important, interiors have been made much safer. Fire-retardant materials have been developed that are replacing older upholstery, carpeting, and side and ceiling panels. The 1984 Air Canada emergency landing at Cincinnati with a fire aboard expedited already ongoing research, development, and installation of the new materials. Also as a result of that accident, more smoke detectors and automatic fire extinguishers have been built into airliner lavatories.

Since dense cabin smoke after that emergency landing (except near the floor) prevented some people from finding exits, new emergency light tracks along one edge of each aisle floor are installed. Small, rectangular white lights show the way, and red lights indicate emergency exit locations. Look at them when you board your plane, even before your flight attendant calls your attention to them in the preflight announcement. Actually, there have been very few inflight fires of any consequence in airline history.

AIRLINE MAINTENANCE AND THE FAA

In the United States, airline maintenance programs must be approved by the Federal Aviation Agency. Most other nations adopt the same strict FAA requirements for their own airlines. The FAA issues guidelines and regulations on which the programs are based. Following program approval, the FAA monitors program performance. Fines are levied for any noncompliance with requirements.

There is a close and good relationship among airlines and the FAA. The FAA is still the policeman, however. Policemen help you to cross a busy street, but they also can arrest you for speeding on that street.

A good relationship also exists worldwide among operators of the various aircraft types and their manufacturers. If one operator, such as an airline, finds a defect or other problem of a noncritical nature on one of its planes, it must notify the FAA—and thus other users and the manufacturers—within twenty-four hours. A service bulletin is then issued, advising all users of what was found and what probably should be done about it. For example: Inspect it, fix it, replace it, and so on, but on a noncompulsory basis.

If it's a more serious situation, an Airworthiness Directive (A.D.) is issued by the FAA. Such a directive outlines a procedure that must be complied with. Again, inspect it, fix it, replace it, and so on, within a certain number of hours, or cycles, or even sooner.

MODERNIZING MAINTENANCE PROGRAMS

Programs in past years were on an inflexible schedule of required inspections and overhauls. As jet aircraft and engines demonstrated their incredible reliability, stamina, and strength, there was a shift to a reliability-centered maintenance concept. To initially establish this concept, two groups of maintenance-related items were identified:

- Those directly affecting safety; these are assigned highest priority for attention.
- Those that are not safety items but that could make the aircraft less available to maintain dependable flight schedules.

These items require continual monitoring of the aircraft.

Today, airline maintenance programs are based on progressive checks and procedures to provide safe, reliable on-time flights. Most airlines and airplanes have similar programs, although with varying specific requirements. Much of the procedure and methodology used to keep a certain type of airliner flying safely and efficiently comes first from the manufacturer, as approved by the FAA. Then the FAA again approves the methods and procedures as written into the airline's program.

Each part of any significance on the airplane has a number. This part, on each individual plane, is tracked through the program, which is computerized on most airlines. Essentially, each part must be checked, changed, or at least inspected in accordance with a schedule. The schedule may be based on each plane's flying hours, on its cycles (a takeoff and landing), or on calendar time. Here are examples:

Unit Name	Type of Schedule
Fuel Boost Pump	No. of Flight Hours
Landing Gear	No. of Cycles
Evacuation Chute	Calendar Time

Some airlines complete all their maintenance, including overhaul of major components, themselves. Others farm it all out to other airlines or to FAA-approved repair companies. Most, however, work with a combination of the options.

Tremendous amounts of money are spent by the airlines on maintenance, whichever route they follow. A recent accounting showed that the average major airline spends more than *$2 million a day* to keep its fleet of planes flying safely.[5] A common misconception about airline maintenance budgets is that the airlines are spending less now than they did prior to deregulation. Actually, it's probably true in some cases—not because the airplanes aren't being as well maintained, but for the following reasons:

- increased efficiency
- modernized procedures
- sophisticated tools
- better manpower utilization
- longer-lasting components
- more use of computers

Aside from the mechanics who handle the progressive maintenance at the various maintenance centers, an airline must provide line maintenance for the various stops on the system. A typical airline provides these types of line maintenance functions:

- Class I: A location where company maintenance personnel are scheduled on duty twenty-four hours a day each day of the week.

- Class II: A location where company maintenance personnel are domiciled but are not scheduled on duty twenty-four hours a day each day of the week.
- Class III: A location where the company contracts for maintenance on a regularly scheduled basis for a portion of each day.
- Class IV: A location where the company contracts for maintenance on an as-required basis or where there is no qualified on-site maintenance available. When a problem occurs, mechanics must be sent to the location.

A typical airline maintenance program uses the following series of inspections and progressive maintenance procedures.

TYPES OF CHECKS AND INSPECTIONS

A walkaround inspection is the lightest of all the inspections made and is done at least once a day. Each flight crew inspects outside and inside the airplane they are to fly before they accept it for a flight. If three crews are to fly the same plane on a given day, there will be at least three walkarounds. Also, a mechanic on the flight line will give still another walkaround check. On an airplane that carries a third cockpit crew member as a flight engineer, an inspection is made at each stop. With just two pilots in the crew, intermediate walkaround inspections are made only if conditions warrant them. As an example, after a wintertime landing in slush, one of the pilots will check certain areas on the airplane for any ingestion of or damage from slush thrown up by the wheels. A portion of the inspection that is done by a flight crew is shown in Figure 8.1.

PREFLIGHT INSPECTION

EXTERIOR INSPECTION (cont'd)

- Fueling Doors - Closed and latched.
- Wing Vent Outlet - Clear (2) places.
- Fuel Leakage Bottom of Wing - Checked, no leaks.
- Tip Ram Air Vent - Clear.
- Main Fuel Vent - Clear.
- Forward & Aft Position Lights (green and white, fixed and oscillating or strobes, if installed) - Lights checks, fairings in tact.
- Wing Landing Light - Retracted, condition good.
- Access cover, top of fin fairing on Vertical Stabilizer - Closed and latched.
- Aileron - Full throw, clear, condition good.
- Aileron Tabs - Condition good, no looseness.
- Fuel Tank Cap - Secured.
- Spoilers - Down and faired.
- Flap Fairings - Attachment secure and no hydraulic leaks.
- Flap Vanes - Condition good (not visible when up).
- Overwing Emergency Exits - Installed and flush.
- Engine Nacelle Floodlight - Condition good.
- Right Main Gear Wheels and Tires - Condition and inflation normal.
- Brakes - No leaks, brake hoses condition good, wear indication checked. (Parking brake must be set to check wear indication.)
- Main Gear Strut - Inflation normal (approximately 2 inches).
- Shimmy Damper - Serviced. Check red line on indicator above REFILL mark.
- Right Main Gear Spray Deflector - Secure, condition good.
- Outboard Main Gear Door - Securely attached, condition good.
- Right Gear Safety Pin - Removed.
- Hydraulic Lines and Electric Conduit - Attached, secured, condition good, no leaks.
- Right Main Gear Door - Closed (after wheel well inspection, spoiler shutoff valve on) (straight up).
- Anti-collision Light (bottom) - Condition good.
- Aft Cargo Compartment Door - Closed and latched.
- Right Engine Inlet Cover - Removed.
- Nacelle Fairing Doors - Closed and latched (4 places).
- Nacelle Inspection Doors - Closed and fastened.
- Nacelle Checked - No leaks.
- Reverser Safety Latch Indicator - Reversers stowed and indicator (red) in recess. (Applies to JT8D-7's only.)
- Right Engine Exhaust Cover - Removed.
- Reverser Safety Pin and Door - Safety pin stowed, lever in normal, cover door closed.
- APU Exhaust Ventilation - Opening clear.
- Rudder Restrictor Pitot Tube - Cover removed.
- Air Conditioning Ram Air Scoop (Vertical Fin) - Clear and unobstructed.
- Top of Fin Fairing on Stabilizer - Fairing down and cover latched.
- Ground Air Conditioning Service Inlet Door - Closed, securely latched.

Figure 8.1. Pilot walkaround inspection.

Inspection and maintenance checks are scheduled between the lightest and heaviest operations; the flight hours at which each is programmed varies with the aircraft type. A transit check is performed at maintenance station overnight stays when no higher check is accomplished. These are scheduled for each 35 hours of flight time. A "thru service A check" each 125 hours ensures the overall condition of the aircraft and its system. A "B service check" approximately each 1,100 hours, "C" checks in four segments of 900 hours each, and heavy D & E maintenance and structural inspections at 20,000 hours keep the planes safely and surely in service. The result is almost a brand-new airplane.

AIRWORTHINESS

During actual programmed maintenance, a mechanic gets an assignment through a card assignment system. The typical job procedure card lists the work to be done, procedures for doing it, and all the descriptive/pictorial data needed to accomplish it. It also includes a sign-off section. The mechanic completes the work; it is then inspected by an airline inspector. Then a maintenance foreman signs off the work and certifies the airplane as *airworthy*.

In addition to the scheduled operations that keep airliners safe and shiny, additional maintenance is done as required. This "as necessary" maintenance is accomplished when determined by mechanic or pilot inspections or by pilots reporting irregularities in the aircraft's logbook.

This FAA-required maintenance performance log is

carried aboard the aircraft. It contains records of problems, corrective action, component replacement, recordings of engine parameters, and like details. It also serves as the input to a carrier's computerized engine monitoring system.

Verbal communication, although used and useful, is not a substitute for a written log entry. The captain of a flight is responsible for complete and correct log entries, although another member of the flight crew may enter them at the captain's bidding. When pilots accept a plane for flight, they check that maintenance "squawks" written up by previous crews have been written off by maintenance and that the aircraft has been certified as airworthy.

A write-off of a pilot complaint may be based on:

1. Immediate correction of the discrepancy.
2. Deferment of a minor item until arrival at maintenance base or until a specified maintenance activity. An airworthiness item cannot be deferred.
3. Use of the Minimum Equipment List (MEL; see following section).

Is it true that, since deregulation of the airlines, airliners are flying around with components not working? That airlines cut costs by not fixing these inoperative units?

When the airlines were deregulated in 1978, safety was not deregulated. Maintenance still follows the conservative policies, procedures, and practices already in place.

Modern transport aircraft provide extensive duplication in systems, components, instrumentation, communications, and structural elements. This duplication is provided to ensure aircraft safety and reliability of service even after failure of certain individual units or certain combinations of units. These features have evolved as a result of extensive efforts spent in research, development, testing, and operations.

Thus, FAA regulations permit the airline's publication of a Minimum Equipment List (MEL) for each aircraft type. This is designed to provide airlines with the guidelines and authority to operate an aircraft with certain items or components inoperative. Each MEL must be approved by the FAA. It will be only if the FAA finds that an acceptable level of safety will be maintained by appropriate operations limitations, by a transfer of the function to another operating component, or by reference to other instruments or components providing the required information.

The MEL can be used to continue operating an aircraft with an inoperative unit only when that unit is listed in MEL manual pages and the captain, dispatcher, and maintenance agree that it would be a safe operation. Figure 8.2 shows a portion of a typical airline's MEL page explaining how the plane could continue in service with a center tank fuel gauge inoperative.

Following approval, the FAA monitors airline use of MEL provisions, especially ensuring that such use is only a temporary expedient to continue flight operation to a point or time when repairs or replacements can be made. Inoperative items are fixed. Flights are safely expedited. Costs are not cut.

QUALITY ASSURANCE

We've seen that inspections abound in connection with airline maintenance. The FAA virtually lives with the carrier, inspecting the programs and inspecting the results of the

MINIMUM EQUIPMENT LIST

SYSTEM AND SEQUENCE NUMBERS	ITEM	1. NUMBER OF UNITS INSTALLED ON AIRCRAFT			
			2. NUMBER REQUIRED FOR DISPATCH		
				3. REMARKS OR EXCEPTIONS	

28 - FUEL

-8	Indicating System, Center Tank	1	0	*(O)	May be inoperative provided fuel is not carried in the center tank.
		1	0	*(O)(M)	May be inoperative provided:

       (1) Both center tank booster pumps are operative, and

       (2) Both main tank quantity systems are operative, and

       (3) The quantity of fuel in the center tank can be determined by sticking the tank or filling the tank or it can be determined that the tank is empty by fuel pump runout (as verified) by main tanks fuel quantity decrease or by fuel used counters.

       See Special Procedure 28-8.

-9	Fuel Tank Totalizing System	1	0	*	May be inoperative.
-10	Dripless Fuel Measuring Sticks	9	0	*(M)	May be inoperative provided:

       (1) Fuel is not carried in center tank, or

       (2) Procedure is followed to positively determine prior to each flight, amount of fuel in affected tank(s), such as other dripstick(s) in the same tank, or by an operative fuel quantity indicating system. (May be accomplished by flight crew or maintenance.

-11	Fueling Panel Fuel Gauges	3	0	*(M)	Any or all may be inoperative provided:

       (1) The fuel quantity in the tanks is determined by using cockpit gages or fuel dripsticks (may be accomplished by flight crew or maintenance), and

       (2) Placard inoperative fueling gages.

Figure 8.2. MEL manual page.

121

programs. And the airline has its own corps of inspectors, who report to a quality assurance, not a maintenance, supervisor.

Both the FAA and airline quality assurance inspectors periodically audit other associated service groups besides those at main airline facilities.

The typical air carrier, for example, thoroughly checks, at least every six months, each vendor that fuels company aircraft. They observe the refueling/defueling operation, the equipment, the safety practices, and knowledge of the vendors' employees, and they check required record keeping.

The airline's own outlying maintenance stations are audited every six months by quality-assurance inspectors. Airlines frequently employ other companies to perform important tasks such as engine or instrument overhaul rather than do it themselves. These are FAA-approved repair stations. They are examined by airline quality-assurance inspectors at least every twelve months. Nothing is left to chance.

Do mechanics try to persuade pilots to accept and fly an aircraft that they know is only marginally safe?

More misinformation is drowned out with a resounding *no*. Mechanics know that people's lives depend on the condition of the aircraft, possibly even their own and family members'. They know that their airlines' reputation, its financial well-being, and its (and their) futures depend on safe operation of flights. This is not to say that they wouldn't discuss with the pilots a situation in the event there was some misunderstanding about a malfunctioning unit and its role in the overall flight system. As with the MEL usage, an alternate operation could be equally suitable and safe.

In addition to safe, every aspect of operations must be legal. When a flight involving maintenance is concerned, the mechanic's name and license and career are on the line. The captain's name and license and career and life are on the line. The captain makes the final determination as to the go/no go status of the flight.

The following paragraphs on maintenance are quoted from "How Safe Is Flying?"—an Air Transport Association pamphlet written by the noted aviation writer Robert J. Serling. These excerpts address the bad press airline maintenance has received in recent years, some of it stemming from FAA fines on carriers.

Even with maintenance modernization, the industry spends more than $4 billion annually on maintenance. Reliability-centered maintenance has improved preventive maintenance and as such it has enhanced U.S. airline safety, not diminished it.

The industry's aircraft dispatch reliability rate has improved steadily since the advent of the jet age nearly 40 years ago—to better than 98 percent. Good maintenance is the cornerstone of dispatch reliability, which is achieved through dedicated hard work, not by using mirrors.

Maintenance-related accidents are rare. In the past 25 years, less than two percent of all fatal crashes were attributed to faulty maintenance—a remarkably reassuring record considering the increasing complexity of airliners themselves and utilization that keeps some flying up to 15 hours a day.

From the recent headlines concerning FAA fines levied against certain airlines, the public may have been given the impression of generally slipshod maintenance throughout the industry. The layman reads or hears about an isolated case of a carrier using improper parts, dispatching flights with inoperative equipment, or faulty record keeping. So what the layman perceives is a badly distorted picture in which isolated incidents, hard to understand or forgive, assume the proportions of an industrywide crisis.

Yet if those incidents are examined dispassionately, they fall far short of being even a minor crisis. Many of the violations were technical in nature, many involving paperwork, and some stemmed from unfortunate human errors such as misreading a parts number. Airlines have taken immediate corrective action in those areas involving airworthiness.

Widely publicized FAA special inspections produced additional distortions. In uncovering occasional sins and lapses from established recordkeeping procedures, the FAA said it found overwhelming compliance with federal maintenance rules and standards.

The very fact that an airline is fined for a maintenance violation tends to obscure the actual nature of that violation. This is not to scoff at or alibi for errors, but rather to point out that many of the supposedly serious violations have raised some eyebrows. One carrier paid a $1,000 fine for each flight of an aircraft that was found to have a crack in the manufacturer's label on a galley—a label listing the maximum weight of items that could be stored in the galley. The fact that the label was still readable didn't impress the FAA inspector.

The violation was not only minor but even petty, yet without giving the details it was included in stories announcing that such-and-such an airline was fined for a series of maintenance violations.

The blunt truth is that the airlines themselves catch more conditions possibly affecting airworthiness than any federal inspection. Typical was the recent case of several widebody jets found to have fuselage frame cracks. They came to light in the course of routine maintenance procedures specifically designed to intercept potential structural problems before they become actual problems. Fuselage inspection is but one part of maintenance, yet the publicity given those cracks was another example of creating a supposed crisis that was no crisis.[6]

The way airliners are designed and built, the way they're maintained—their care and feeding—these ensure you a safe flying journey.

What we have covered in this chapter is typical of airlines in the United States and also of most of the world's air carriers.

A Thought to Fly by

Airline airplanes are strongly built and well maintained. They're safe.

CHAPTER 9

You're Ready, You're Set, Let's Go!

It's time to take a flight!

Some anxiety at this point is natural—you're trusting us and our experience that our methods will work. Until you actually use them up in the air, you won't know for sure.

Many of the people in our classes still have some anxiety or doubt when they board the plane for the graduation flight. But they do get on, despite their doubts, and we get many letters from former class members thanking us for encouraging them to stay on the plane and give it a chance.

You're not the same person you were before reading this book and practicing the relaxation and thought stopping. You can't possibly act the way you did on previous flights. You now have two of the best tools available to fight anxiety. You have them right in your carry-on bag, purse, or briefcase to take with you on every flight.

Remember, you can put up with *anything* for a short time, and those horrible feelings you get when you're anxious will not hurt you. It's very frightening when you get those physical symptoms and your heart is pounding so hard that it feels as if it's coming right through your chest wall. But you're not going to have a heart attack; you're not going to pass out; you're not going to go crazy. The sooner you remember this, the sooner those feelings will lose their importance and leave.

A Thought to Fly by

Feelings of anxiety are very uncomfortable, but they are not dangerous to you physically or mentally.

We've never had a single person on any of our graduation flights have a heart attack, pass out, or go crazy, and we've taken thousands of graduates up into the air. We always tell the class members on the first night that we have no qualms whatsoever about taking every one of them on that graduation flight if they come to the classes and practice their relaxation exercises. We know the methods work. If they thought that we would take thirty-five to forty fearful flyers up in an airplane for one hour if our methods didn't work, they'd have to be crazy. There are easier ways to make a living!

PLANNING A TRIP

The flight should be about forty-five minutes to one hour in duration, and that means each way—you do have to get back again. It should be long enough so you have time to get over any initial anxiety and put the methods to work, but not so long that it seems overwhelming.

Often people want to take this trip alone to try out their wings. If you do decide to take someone with you, don't take another fearful flyer; he or she will have all kinds of horror stories you might not have even thought about. Rather, pick an understanding and encouraging friend. Explain your relaxation exercises and thought stopping, and your friend won't bother you when you're concentrating. Your friend can also serve as an active thought stopper by talking to you, playing cards with you, or otherwise keeping you occupied.

If you don't have the time or money to take a practice flight but have another flight coming up anyway, that's fine. The important thing is to fly as soon as you can after reading our book and implementing the four-week plan outlined in Chapter 7. Our methods work just as well for longer flights. We graduated a class in Washington, D.C., on a Saturday afternoon, and on Sunday one of the members, Dan, left for South Africa. And Dan had not flown for seven years. In fact, he could not even look at a plane in the sky without becoming anxious. His business partner called us on Monday and said that Dan had called from London, after completing the first leg of his journey, and reported that the flight had been great. He went on to South Africa without any problems and has flown many times since.

BUYING YOUR TICKET

If you purchase your ticket several weeks to a month in advance, you have a better chance of getting your choice of dates and times. An excellent time to do it might be at the same time you begin the four-week plan.

A good travel agent can also help you get the best fares and times to travel. But, whether an agent is buying the tickets or you are, make sure you get answers to all your questions and concerns. Most airline reservation agents are used to answering questions and are courteous and patient, but if you happen to get one who is not, ask to talk with the supervisor. Airlines want your business and want you to be a satisfied customer.

Try not to travel at peak times. Avoid flying the days before and after holidays, summer weekends, or early mornings and late afternoons, which are crowded with business travelers. You want to keep yourself as calm and relaxed as possible, so the fewer lines you have to wait on and the less crowded the planes are, the better you will feel. A late-morning flight is great, as you won't have all day to think about it.

SELECTING YOUR SEAT

Most airlines allow you to choose your seat weeks in advance. Take advantage of this and pick a seat in which you are going to feel comfortable. If you're claustrophobic, choose an aisle seat near the front of the plane. You'll have an open area on at least one side and can get up and walk around without climbing over people. If you're near the front of the plane, you won't have to look up that long, narrow aisle or wait very long to get off the plane once you've landed. You're also nearer to where some of the flight attendants sit and spend most of their time. You can ask them questions about any sounds you hear or just chat with them when they aren't busy.

Claustrophobics may feel better flying during the day than at night. Darkness often makes people feel even *more* closed in. If you have a fear of heights, however, you probably won't want to sit by a window and won't care if it's light or dark outside. You might prefer the dark, because then you can't see how high up you are!

Ask the reservation agent about the size of the plane and where the engines are located. If you like large planes better than small ones, or vice-versa, try to arrange your schedule accordingly. If you don't like hearing those engine noises, don't sit near the engines; if you don't like watching those wings move or the wing flaps go up and down, don't sit near them. You do have choices.

Fearful flyers always ask us about the *safest* place to sit. Even though many people think more people survive airline crashes if they are in the back of the plane, this isn't necessarily true. For every accident where someone survived who was sitting in the back, another one had survivors in the front of the plane. Besides, since the percentage of airline accidents is so low, you shouldn't choose your seat based on the possibility of crashing.

Some people ask us to recommend the best place to sit in the airplane so as to feel the least movement during turbulence. You may want to sit over the wings, as you may feel the movement of the plane somewhat less. But it doesn't make a great deal of difference where you sit.

OTHER CONCERNS

Some people experience a slight "popping" feeling in their ears during the descent of the plane. This feeling is due to an increase of atmospheric pressure against the eardrum as the plane descends. Yawning, swallowing, chewing gum, or sucking on hard candy helps to alleviate any discomfort. If these things do not help, you might try taking an over-the-counter decongestant about one hour prior to takeoff and one hour prior to landing (or follow the directions on the box). If you have a severe cold or sinus condition, you might want to postpone flying until the condition has cleared up. If you have chronic ear problems, talk with your doctor about the flight.

If you don't get motion sickness in cars or on boats, you are not likely to get it on an airplane. In fact, even some people who do get queasy in cars or on boats do not experience any similar difficulty when flying. Most flights are relatively smooth, and with the sophisticated weather radar that we now have it is usually possible to get around or above the turbulence. But if you do experience motion sickness, there are many over-the-counter products to help you. Ask your pharmacist about the best ones. However, be sure to take only the prescribed dosage. One woman, on one of our graduation flights, felt that if one dose would help, three would be even better. The medicine itself made her sick during the entire flight.

THE DAY BEFORE THE FLIGHT

Try to keep the day before the flight as free from stress as you can. This is your day to get everything organized and to prepare your body and mind for the flight.

Here is a list of essentials to pack in your carry-on bag:

- Relaxation tape, cassette player, earplugs, and extra batteries.

- Note card with four thought stoppers on it, and an extra rubber band.
- Cassettes of your favorite music.
- Active thought stoppers—books, playing cards, crossword puzzles, knitting, paperwork.
- Gum, hard candy, decongestant.
- Motion-sickness medication if needed.
- A sweater or lightweight jacket (the airplane may not be as warm as you'd like).

Check your tickets, lay out the clothing you will be wearing, and do any other packing that is necessary.

To prepare your body and mind:

- Do the relaxation exercises at least twice: once in the morning and before retiring. Do them at other times as often as necessary.
- Stop every fearful or negative thought about flying. Make another note card with your four thought stoppers on it and keep it close by you. Of course, you're wearing your rubber band.
- Do something enjoyable and try not to start any new or stressful projects at work or home. Don't have too many last-minute errands to run.
- Go to bed early enough to get a good night's sleep, but not so early that you won't be tired. Play the tape; it's great if you have difficulty sleeping. However, don't panic if you can't sleep. Read a book, watch television, and relax.

A Thought to Fly by

Some anxiety is natural—you haven't tried the methods out yet. It may even be excitement you're feeling.

THE BIG DAY

Allow yourself plenty of time on the day of the flight to get to the airport, get your seat assignment (if you don't already have one), and board the plane. Remember, if you are worried about being late, finding a parking space, or anything else, you will become anxious. Your body won't know what you're anxious about; it will just start to get those old feelings of anxiety. You will begin to feel the way you did when you were anxious about flying, whether you still are or not. If you are flying at a time when you cannot avoid being "stressed" or anxious about something else in your life, try to keep the anxiety where it belongs. Don't automatically think you're anxious about flying and pin the blame on the airplane.

Call the airline ahead of time to see if your flight is going to leave on time. It's better to know in advance if there's going to be a delay.

You've already been to the airport several times during the last month (if you completed the four-week plan), so you should know the route well, how long it takes, and the best place to park. Plan to arrive at least an hour before your flight is scheduled to depart. If driving isn't one of your favorite things to do, ask a friend or relative to take you. You can then chat or listen to your tape on the way.

AT THE AIRPORT

If you haven't picked up your tickets yet, you will need to do so at the ticket counter. Also, if you have any luggage that needs to be checked, you can do that at a curbside check-in or the ticket counter. Again, feel free to ask any questions. If you already have your ticket and no baggage to check, you can proceed directly to the gate area.

Everyone going to the gate area must first go through security. Security is sometimes frightening to fearful flyers because they are now aware that people and carry-on luggage are being checked for weapons or other dangerous items. But try to think of it in a positive way (thought stopping) and realize that the security people seldom find any weapons and, even if they do, the people are not carrying them in order to hijack the plane. Besides, if the weapon is found, it won't be allowed on the plane.

Security will ask you to place everything you are carrying on a conveyor belt. These articles will pass under an X ray machine. You will then be instructed to walk under an archway that will detect any metal objects on your person. Don't be alarmed if the alert buzzer goes off on you or someone else. Keys, money, jewelry, computers, and even metal leg braces can cause the alarm to sound.

When you reach the gate area, go up to the counter and get a boarding pass if you have not done so at the ticket counter. If you have taken our advice to arrive in plenty of time, you should now be able to sit down and relax. Listen to your relaxation tape one more time. You don't have to actually do the exercises—just listening to them will signal your body to relax (if you've been practicing the exercises faithfully). Other people will think you are listening to music. If the plane is delayed, listen to the tape as often as necessary. (You can't be *too* relaxed.) If it's a long delay, don't just sit there and fret—take a walk, go to the bookstore, buy a soft drink. Movement helps alleviate tension. Use your thought stoppers.

BOARDING THE PLANE

The aircraft probably will be boarded by rows, starting from the rear of the plane and working up to the front. You may wish to wait until everyone else has boarded before you get on. You can't get on before your row is called, but you can certainly get on after it's called. If you wait, you don't have to stand in the jetway or the aisle of the plane waiting for the people in front of you to stow their luggage and find their seats. You might as well sit in the gate area and relax until all the congestion has cleared.

If you've never flown, you need to know that there probably is a short tunnel, called a jetway, connecting the terminal building with the airplane. That way people avoid having to go outside to board the plane; this is especially convenient if it's raining or snowing. If you have waited until the other passengers have boarded, you will just sail through the jetway in a minute or so and be at the door of the plane.

As you enter the plane, you will find a flight attendant or two waiting to greet you. You might want to tell them that you are not a comfortable flyer. If they are alerted to this fact now, they can stop by later to see how you are doing, and you will feel comfortable in calling them over to ask questions. Ask them if you can look into the cockpit and meet the pilots. The pilots love their jobs, are proud of their aircraft, and like the chance to meet their passengers, an opportunity they don't often get. They may even make more announcements during the flight if they know they have a timid flyer aboard. And you will know that there are at least two normal-looking, real-live people up there behind that closed cockpit door.

When you get to your seat, stow your carry-on bag either in the overhead compartment or under the seat in front of you. Put as little underneath the seat in front of you as possible; leave room to stretch out your legs, and you will feel less crowded. Loosen any tight clothing, kick off your shoes, and get comfortable. Take out your tape player, your note cards, one of your books, your knitting, or whatever you want to do to keep busy. There is a pocket on the back of the seat in front of you that you can put things into. There may be a magazine or two in it as well as a small bag to use in case of air sickness.

If you're starting to feel a little anxious, listen to your tape. You won't have to listen to it this much on other flights, but remember that your goal this time is to get a good flight under your belt. This will make your other flights much easier because you will know it can be done. Most airlines do not allow passengers to operate a tape player during taxi, takeoff, or landing; this is so that passengers can listen to safety instructions and any additional announcements that may be necessary. But even if takeoff is a bad time for you, you can play the tape right beforehand, and your relaxed feeling will last through the takeoff. You can listen to it again as soon as you are airborne. If the flight attendant asks you to remove your earplugs at any other time, make sure he or she knows that you are listening to a tape player and not a radio. Passengers are not allowed to play radios during a flight because they may interfere with aircraft navigation systems.

Over your head is a passenger service panel with a light, a flight attendant call button, and an airflow dial. Fearful flyers sometimes worry that they can't breathe or get enough air on airplanes. Turn the airflow button and direct the cool stream of air on you. If you are unable to operate any of these buttons, ask the flight attendant to assist you.

DURING THE FLIGHT

If you start to feel anxious during the flight, close your eyes, take a few deep breaths, and picture yourself at home. Let your body feel the way it does when you have just finished doing the exercises in your favorite chair.

Don't sit rigidly in the seat, hanging on to the arms. Keep your body loose and periodically "shake out" your arms and legs. Later, when the "Fasten Seat Belts" sign goes off, get up and walk around. Walk to the rest room even if you don't need to. Movement helps release tension.

JOINING FORCES WITH THAT AIRPLANE

Most fearful flyers become frightened when the plane makes any sudden movement such as banking or turning or moving up and down during turbulence. Our hope is that after reading the information in this book, you will not be so frightened, but you still must teach your body to react differently to these things. The fearful flyer automatically tenses his or her body at any unfamiliar sound or movement—exactly the opposite of what we want you to do. We now want movements and noises to become the signal for you to *relax* your body even more. You can retrain your body to behave the way you want it to behave.

We want you to now feel that you are connected to that airplane. For example, if it's a 727, you are now an added piece of the 727. This means when that 727 banks to the right, you lean to the right. (Don't lean *against* the bank.)

When the plane moves up and down during turbulence, don't fight this movement—move up and down with it. You don't have a choice—you're now connected to the plane. If you don't fight the motion, you won't notice it nearly as much. You may also feel more in control if you're part of that wonderful flying machine.

The "Old" You On An Airplane

STIMULUS	RESPONSE
Sudden movements or noises	"Oh my God, what is wrong now?" (Tense every muscle in your body and hang on for dear life!)

The "New" You on an Airplane

Sudden movements or noises	Slump back into the seat. Lower your shoulders and let your body go more and more limp.

Use thought stopping during the flight. Take out your note card and look at it often. Every time you have a fearful thought or feel anxious, *stop* that thought immediately and think about one of the things on your card. You will break up that anxiety, lower it, or make it go away entirely. Even if it comes back, it will have to start all over again—and you can just zap it again. You can't think of two things at the same time; you decide what thoughts will make you feel more comfortable. You have the control.

Don't be alarmed if feelings of anxiety try to come back. Your body and mind will try to trick you and make you feel just the way you did before you read this book and completed the four-week plan. You can't possibly be that same person. You have new information and new tools to help you fly comfortably. No one can ever take them away from you.

CHAPTER 10

The Plane's Ready, The Plane's Set, Let's Go!

You've done all the things you were asked to do in preparing for this flight, and so have the cockpit crew and the cabin crew. The things they have done are detailed in the policies and procedures sections of their manuals and in the regulations of the government and of their airline. What has been going on with them and the airplane?

THE CREW IN OPERATIONS

Your flight's crew members report to the airline's operations office at least an hour prior to departure time. They first read all notices and flight information bulletins that have been issued since their last flight and make all necessary revisions to their manuals. Their manuals are periodically checked for being up to date.

The pilots familiarize themselves with weather conditions, using hourly sequence reports and forecasts, weather maps, and winds aloft and temperature reports and forecasts. Reports or forecasts of icing, thunderstorms, wind shear, and any other weather conditions are considered in planning the flight, as are field conditions—the condition of the surface of airport runways, taxiways, and ramps.

HOW MUCH FUEL IS NEEDED?

In conjunction with the flight's dispatcher, the required amount of fuel to be loaded is computed. For U.S. domestic flights, there must be enough fuel to fly to the airport to which the airplane is dispatched; thereafter, to fly to and land at the most distant listed alternate airport; and thereafter, to cruise for an additional forty-five minutes. The rules for extended flight outside the United States are more complicated; they specify amounts that provide equivalent safety reserves.

The first officer prepares a flight plan/clearance form for the flight. (There are as many names for such a form as there are airlines.) When it is complete, typically it will have attached to it, for use in flight, at least:

- a computerized flight plan (if applicable)
- a copy of the latest available hourly weather reports for en route and alternate airports
- a copy of the latest available terminal forecasts
- a copy of wind direction and velocity and temperatures at all altitudes
- a copy of the latest government-issued NOTAMs (Notices To Airmen)

The flight dispatcher, who shares responsibility with the captain for the safe conduct of the flight, forwards a flight release to the captain. (See Chapter 6 for details.) The captain and the dispatcher must agree that each phase of the flight can be conducted safely.

While the pilots are doing their things in the operations office, the flight attendants are doing theirs. They read the information letters and briefing bulletins that pertain to their duties aboard the flight. They, too, have manuals to revise. They check for such items pertaining to their flight as changes in routine stops, expected weather conditions en route, any weather delays, expected turbulence, and so on. The captain briefs them, either as a group or through the senior flight attendant.

INSPECTING THE PLANE

The flight attendants board the plane at least thirty minutes prior to the scheduled departure time and prepare to receive their passengers. An important early duty is to check, in conjunction with cockpit crew members, all the cabin emergency equipment (first-aid kits, fire extinguishers, portable oxygen bottles, flashlights, megaphones, life vests, rafts) for condition, currency, and proper storage. They also check the inflatable escape slides, which are mounted on doors used for emergency evacuation of the aircraft. They must each have a personal flashlight.

They also check for all required cabin furnishings and galley equipment and call for maintenance or catering if either is necessary. If there were problems or discrepancies on the inbound flight of this plane, the inbound crew will have reported them, and the problems should already have been solved.

A flight engineer, after obtaining pertinent weather and fuel-loading information, proceeds to the aircraft for the necessary pre-flight checks. The pilots complete the remainder of their operations office duties and then go to the plane at least fifteen minutes prior to departure. On those types of planes that have super-sophisticated nagivation and/or fuel management systems, it is necessary to allot more time to the setting up of the systems' computers. The days of the goggled, white-scarved aviator who clambered into his loaded biplane a minute before departure time and yelled, "Crank 'er up, I'm ready for takeoff," are long gone.

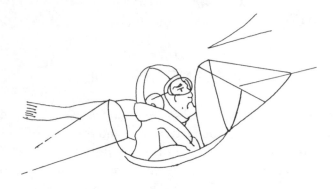

A WALKAROUND INSPECTION

By this time, at least one of the flight crew members has performed a walkaround inspection of the airplane, probably prior to your boarding it. The airplane you'll fly on has been checked and prepared as thoroughly as practicable so as to ensure your safety and comfort during the flight. (Refer to pages 116–18 for details on the inspections.)

If you're flying in wintertime conditions, de-icing of the plane's surface may take place. The captain is not permitted to take off if snow or ice is adhering to any critical part of the plane. Your airplane may be de-iced while it's loading for departure on the ramp, or it may taxi or be towed to a more remote area for spraying with an ethylene glycol solution. Brushes and squeegees may also be used. The glycol not only removes frozen accumulations but also prevents additional precipitation from sticking to the surfaces for some time. If a sufficiently long ground delay occurs before takeoff, the de-icing procedure may have to be repeated. Modern airliners have their own anti-icing and/or de-icing systems that are very effective while in flight but not operable when the plane is on the ground.

The flight crew then completes an acceptance cockpit checklist consisting of numerous challenge and response items ensuring that all systems and equipment items on the aircraft are ready for engine start and flight. Next, a "before start" checklist is completed. The flight crew then pauses until receiving a signal from the ground that they should start the engines. With everybody and everything on board, with passenger, service, and cargo compartment doors securely latched closed, it's "Clear to start engines, sir!"

LEAVING THE GATE

Planes leave the gate in three different manners, depending on the airline, the airplane type, the airport, the particular gate at the airport, and ramp conditions at that gate. The ways to go are to taxi out, be pushed back, or to power back.

Taxi out
Engine power is used to taxi away from the gate.

Pushback

A powerful tug is connected to the plane's nosewheel assembly. On proper signal coordination between the cockpit and a ground signaler, the tug pushes the airplane backward and maneuvers it into a proper position to begin taxiing away from the ramp on its own engine power. The aircraft's engines may be started during the pushback or after the pushback has been completed.

Powerback

The plane is taxied backward, using its own engine thrust, reversed, to leave the gate.

In each case, when the plane is finally released to continue under its own power, it is done with a smart salute from the ground agent controlling the move.

THE FLIGHT PLAN

The flight plan filed with Air Traffic Control for each airline flight contains certain information and certain proposals. The information includes the flight number, type of aircraft, and the estimated time en route.

The plan proposes that the flight leave the airline's gate at a certain time. (The time used was formerly called Greenwich Mean Time. It's now termed Coordinated Universal Time.) It proposes that the airplane operate at certain flight levels and follow specified routes.

Mostly prior to but no later than departing from the terminal ramp, the flight crew requests by radio an ATC flight clearance to the next point of landing.

THE ATC CLEARANCE

The response contains the ATC clearance from the area's air-traffic control center. If the pilot's proposals can be coordinated into the traffic situation existent at that time, the request for clearance could be answered as in this typical example: "USAir 516, this is Cleveland Center, cleared as filed." Then there would follow instructions for leaving the airport and entering into the protected airspace, such as "Maintain runway heading to 5,000 feet, turn right to a heading of three six zero, climb to and maintain 7,000 feet. Expect further clearance to flight level three two zero 10 minutes after departure. Contact departure control on one two zero point one five [120.15 megahertz]. Squawk five one three zero [transponder or radar beacon code setting]."

The first officer, who will have been jotting down the clearance in a form of shorthand, now repeats it verbatim. This readback of the clearance cross checks that it was correctly received and understood to the satisfaction of the ATC controller and each cockpit crew member. Also, the clearance and the readback are now tape recorded at the sender's site and in the cockpit, the latter on a thirty-minute continuous tape.

If the flight's proposed altitude(s) or routing(s) does not fit into the present traffic situation, a different clearance will be issued. Instead of "cleared as filed," each point of the routing, each altitude to be climbed and descended to would be specified.

While the plane is taxiing out for takeoff, the cabin crew is busy making certain that everything and everyone is set to go. The crew up front is busy too, with the before-takeoff checklist—but it's an orderly, not a rushed, busy. (See Figure 10.1.)

P/N 1B1133693-1   C/C 177-1774

COCKPIT CHECKLIST
NORMAL PROCEDURES
B-727-200A

BEFORE START

Altimeters, Flt. Insts.	CHKD & SET
Engine Instruments	CHKD & SET
Fuel, Oil, Hyd. Quantities -- CHKD,	LBS.
OMEGA	SET
PDCS	SET
ACARS	SET

▶

Fuel Panel	SET FOR START
Hydraulics	SET FOR START
Cabin Pressure Panel	SET
Seat Belt/No Smoking	ON
Anti-Collision Lights	ON
Parking Brake, Pressure	ON & CHKD
A/C Packs, Pressure	OFF, PSI
Galley Power	OFF

AFTER START

Engine Anti-Ice	AS REQUIRED
Hydraulics	"A" SYSTEM PRESSURIZED
Door Lights & Lock	CHKD
Galley Power	ON
Radar	TEST/WX

BEFORE TAKEOFF

Shoulder Harness	FASTENED
Takeoff Data	CHKD & SET
Stabilizer & Trim Tabs	SET FOR T.O.
Ice Protection	AS REQUIRED
Probe Heaters	ON & CHKD
Yaw Dampers	ON & CHKD
HSI Selector	N/L
Electrical	NO LIGHTS ESS PWR #
Fuel Panel	SET FOR T.O.
Air Conditioning & Press.	SET FOR T.O.
Flight Controls	CHKD FREE
Flaps	°, GREEN LIGHT, DETENT
APU	OFF

▶

Anti-Skid	ON
Ignition	ON
Flight Recorder	CHKD/ON
Transponder	ON
Auto-Pack Trip	NORMAL

AFTER TAKEOFF

Ignition	AS REQUIRED
Auto-Pack Trip Switch	CUTOUT
Fuel	AS REQUIRED
Hydraulics - PRESSURE & QUANTITIES NORMAL	
Air Conditioning & Press.	CHKD & SET

PRELIMINARY LANDING

Air Cond., Press. & Cooling Doors	SET
Fuel Panel	SET FOR LANDING
Brake Pressure	CHKD
Hydraulics - PRESSURE & QUANTITIES NORMAL	
Landing Data	CHKD, BUGS SET
HSI Selector	N/L
Altimeters	SET
Shoulder Harness	FASTENED

FINAL LANDING

Seat Belt/No Smoking	ON
Auto-Brakes	AS DESIRED
Ice Protection	AS REQUIRED
Ignition	ON
Gear	DOWN, LIGHTS CHKD
Anti-Skid	ON
Speed Brakes	AS REQUIRED

▶

Flaps	° GREEN LIGHT

AFTER LANDING

Flaps	AS REQUIRED
Speed Brakes	FORWARD, IN DETENT
Stabilizer Trim	AS REQUIRED
Anti-Skid	OFF
Auto-Brakes	OFF
Ignition	OFF
Ice Protection	AS REQUIRED
Flt.Recdr,Transpdr,Radar,DME,Omega	STBY OR OFF
Air Cond. & Press.	SET AS REQUIRED/GND

PARKING AND SECURING

Parking Brake	AS REQUIRED
APU	ON BUS
Start Levers	CUTOFF
Anti-Collision Lights	OFF
Electrical	EXT/APU
Fuel Panel	SET AS REQUIRED
Hydraulics	SET AS REQUIRED
Air Cond. & Press.	SET AS REQUIRED

PRECEDING ITEMS TO BE COMPLETED
EACH STOP, FOLLOWING ITEMS AT
TERMINATION ONLY.

Stabilizer Trim	0°
Emergency Exit Lights	OFF
Electrical	AS REQUIRED
Battery Switch	AS REQUIRED

FAA APPROVED - Date NOV 1 7 1987

Principal Air Carrier Operations
Inspector EA - FSDO - 19

Figure 10.1. Before-takeoff checklist.

The flight attendants finish up their departure announcements over the P.A. system. They explain the use of seat belts, door and window exits, oxygen, flotation devices, and more. For the most part their message is rigidly adhered to in order to ensure that it is complete and legal for the FAA and for the airline company. But experienced flight attendants sometimes do deviate somewhat in words and style. They do this not only to make the message more interesting but also to try to get passengers to listen. Even the newer-technology presentations on television or movie screens get scant attention.

What you'd learn from listening and looking could save your life if the very improbable—an emergency situation—suddenly occurred. Those who are old hands at air travel are actually listening and looking.

NOISES AND THOSE NOISY TAKEOFFS

You might have heard the wing flaps and any leading edge devices being positioned for the coming takeoff. Other noises you might hear while taxiing are wheel brakes squealing or engine sounds changing, especially on propjet aircraft. The next noises—all normal sounds—will occur during and following takeoff.

Taxiing along, passengers may see lighted signs pointing the pilots' way to taxiways. They use letters (A,B, or C) to identify taxiways. Blue lights along the pavement edges or green lights in the center indicate that they *are* taxiways.

Runways are identified by their magnetic compass headings, printed on cockpit charts, painted on runway ends, and seen often on direction signs similar to those for taxiways. For instance, Runway 27 indicates a runway heading west, or 270°. Since runways are used in both directions, the opposite end will have a 9 painted on it to indicate 90 degrees compass heading east. If three north runways are provided, parallel to one another, one will be labeled 36L, one 36C (for center), and one 36R.

Runway lighting at night varies considerably, depending on the amount of traffic and how low weather conditions could be with its use. Minimum illumination consists of white runway edge lights. These lights turn to amber as the plane goes farther down the runway. With higher-rated runways, centerline lights and touchdown zone lights are added. Pilots landing on that runway, when visibility and cloud ceilings are low, first see a string of approach lights with sequenced flashing lights that say, in effect, "Follow me to the runway." Green lights extend across the runway threshold as a "welcome" sign. At the far end, red lights across the runway warn against going farther (even though there are overrun areas).

As the plane taxis close to the takeoff runway, the first officer switches from Ground Control to Tower communications frequency and reports that the flight is ready for takeoff. Depending on other traffic—either ahead awaiting takeoff or in the landing pattern—the pilots might be told to either stand by, to taxi into position (for takeoff) and hold, or that they are cleared for takeoff.

Flight attendants are advised (through bell signals or by a cabin announcement from the cockpit) that takeoff is imminent and they should take their various stations and fasten their seat belts.

As the flight moves onto the takeoff runway, the transponder beacon is dialed onto the assigned frequency. Controllers know they're viewing USAir 33 on their screens along with all the other blips.

The takeoff can be made by the captain or by the co-pilot. The captain designates the pilot flying and the pilot not flying for each leg of the trip. Even after the control tower has cleared the flight onto the runway, both pilots search the approach path for any aerial traffic before moving into takeoff position. This cautious cross checking is bred into airline pilots. It extends into all phases of flight under Air Traffic Control. When a flight is solidly in cloud, pilots cannot see other traffic, but they listen for what is going on around them. This creates situation awareness that cross checks an already good and effective system. In clear air, even though under positive control, airline pilots have a logical and a legal requirement to watch out for other aircraft.

Once the flight has been cleared for takeoff and lined up in the center of the runway, and before takeoff checks and crew briefings have been completed, the captain advances thrust levers to the computed takeoff power setting. Cockpit crew members cross check all engine instruments to monitor that takeoff power is set. The first officer calls out the various speeds (V1, Vr, V2) as they're attained, conforming to standard procedure.

The plane lifts off, and the landing gear is retracted. This will make the first significant noise heard on any plane immediately after takeoff. Almost every airliner retracts its wheels at this time, so fearful flyers can remember that this is what that noise is. Fearful flyers shouldn't try to exactly memorize the sound because (1) the sound is different depending on where they're sitting and (2) the sound is different on different types of planes.

What actually happens? Most planes' main wheels and nose wheels retract with hydraulic pressure: First a down-lock is released, then doors open up and the airflow noise around the doors increases. The various sets of wheels (a minimum of three) retract and are locked up, and the doors re-close. A number of things happen in sequence amid a number of noises. Don't worry about what you hear. There is very little that goes wrong with modern-day planes' landing gear mechanisms.

The next noise(s) are those of wing flaps and any wing leading edge devices retracting. This could be done all at once or, more likely, in two or three separate stages as airspeed increases.

NOISE ABATEMENT TAKEOFFS

Airliners in the United States today make so-called "noise abatement takeoffs" every takeoff. The idea is to get away from the airport and surroundings as quickly and quietly as practicable. At some airports, turns shortly after takeoff are required to avoid noise-sensitive areas. Pilots make these turns with due consideration for flight safety and without banking the plane any more than during any flight maneuver.

Contrary to uncomfortable flyers' tales about really steep turns and steep climbs they've endured or heard about, turns and climbs are fairly standard with airlines worldwide.

- After takeoff, the initial climb angle: 15 degrees above the horizon (some planes require 20 degrees).
- Turning: 25 degrees *normal* maximum bank, 30 degrees *maximum*.
- On landing approach: varying from 2 to 5 degrees below the horizon to 2 degrees above.

The only other noises one might hear during the climbing, cruising, or descending phases of a flight are those of increases or decreases in engine power settings and occasional bells or chimes. After takeoff, engine sound decreases as power is reduced for climb; it decreases slightly again when cruise power is set. Most passengers are not aware of these changes. There's no need to be.

Passengers shouldn't be concerned about the chimes often heard during various phases of flights. They're mostly cabin or cockpit service calls. If a bell signal must be used to signal an emergency situation, passengers are advised. There are no secret signals used to indicate an emergency. In fact, there are probably no two airlines that use the same chime system. Also, different types of aircraft may or may not sound chimes when seat belt/no-smoking signs turn on or off. In other words, don't be fearful about those pleasant-sounding chimes.

FLIGHT AND LANDING

Flight crews use various navigation charts to fly between cities. The en route charts are like the road maps you use on auto trips. (See Figure 10.2.) One important addition is the minimum altitudes specified for each section of the flight. The roads laid out for our sky travel are lines connecting VOR (Visual Omni Range) radio navigation stations. Networks of VORs blanket the United States; in fact, they blanket most of the world. These, plus radio beacons, permit airplanes, big and small, to navigate over the world's land routes. More sophisticated navigation systems—Loran, Omega, and Inertial Navigational Systems—

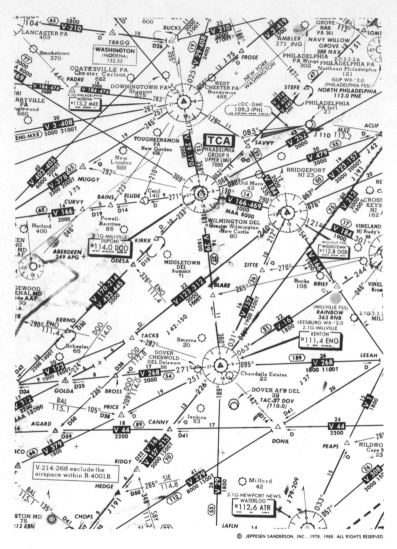

Figure 10.2. En route navigation chart.

permit transoceanic flight in addition to precise passage over land areas.

Aircraft can fly airways—the lines connecting two radio stations—or they can fly directly between two geographic points if ATC can handle them that way, consistent with other traffic. ATC makes every effort to accommodate flights to save time and fuel or to avoid turbulent air.

For example, let's say that on our flight the weather had been quite good on departure, but the destination, Philadelphia, has had low cloud ceiling and restricted visibility most of the day. As the flight nears Philadelphia, the co-pilot radios "in range," meaning ten to fifteen minutes from landing. This communication is on "company frequency," the airline's own communication system. The airline operations agent advises that weather conditions there consist of a one-hundred-foot overcast ceiling with runway visibility measured at 1,400 feet. There's a light wind from the east. With those weather conditions, the pilot can make an instrument landing system (ILS) approach to land on Runway 9 right.

A few miles out, ATC "hands over" the flight to approach control; now the pilots communicate with those controllers at the airport.

The flight attendants are advised when the flight is about ten minutes out and descending through 10,000 feet. An "inbound sterile cockpit" is in effect; it was in place for takeoff and initial climb also. This means no unnecessary communications from the cabin, no conversation in the cockpit except as necessary for approach and landing procedures. F/As make their arrival announcements, which include the requirements that seat backs and trays be in their up (locked) position and that carry-on luggage be restowed if necessary.

The pilots review all aspects of the ILS 9R approach—minimum altitudes, frequencies, glideslope height at the outer market, missed approach procedure, and so on. They review these together even if they know them by heart, even if they've already used the procedure twice today. They also compute approach and landing speeds; this is all part of completing the preliminary landing checklist.

As the plane descends into approach, passengers may hear some additional noises. Engine power is decreased; there'll still be outside air sounds, though, as the plane passes through the air ocean at still-high speeds (even as high as 250 knots below 10,000 feet). Wing flaps are lowered in stages—various approach settings and the landing setting. At the landing setting, slight buffeting may be transmitted to the cabin. This is normal.

Slight buffeting, which is normal, may also be felt as speed brake panels are raised into the air flowing over the top of the wings to slow the plane down. These, on most planes, are used only prior to the wing flaps' being lowered. After landing, they are called spoilers, and they are raised again this time to spoil the lift of the wings. This causes the plane to settle more firmly onto the ground, and the wheel brakes are more effective. The noise of the landing gear being lowered is heard shortly before landing, the same noises as heard after takeoff. (Up locks released, doors opening and closing, wheels locking down, and so on.)

Incidentally, whenever a plane is making a non-normal landing or an unscheduled landing (such as returning to land after a departure during which a door turns out to be not securely locked), airport emergency equipment will be waiting adjacent to the landing runway. It is a requirement that fire trucks, ambulances, and other emergency equipment be there in the unlikely event they are needed. It's

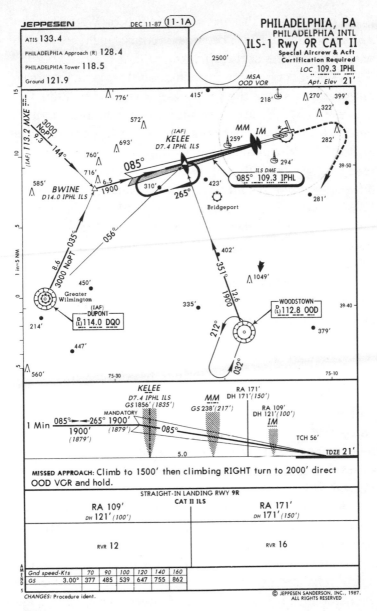

Figure 10.3. A cockpit approach.

good practice for the airport crews, too. We know that some fearful flyers have been quite concerned when they've seen such vehicles at the airport.

During a typical approach procedure, one pilot calls out altitudes above the ground. For example: 1,000 feet, 500 feet, 200 feet, 100 feet, and so on. The pilot looking outside is ready to land the plane if the runway environment is identified; the pilot flying or controlling the autopilot is ready to go around if it is not. (Different airlines use different procedures.) If a go-around is made, it's just like a takeoff, except that it starts above instead of on the runway. Go-arounds are not dangerous; pilots practice them during training and checking, starting from fifty feet above the ground.

In our example case, though, the flight into Philadelphia, the runway came in sight straight ahead as the plane reached 200 feet on its descent. A normal, smooth landing was made.

There are times when the pilot doesn't concentrate on making the super-smooth landing that passengers like and judge pilots on. If the runway is slippery or relatively short (but always within legal limits), the pilot "puts the airplane on"—that is, he or she touches down firmly, raises the lift spoilers, and shortly applies reverse thrust and wheel braking. Braking is more effective when tires are solidly on the runway.

Reverse engine thrust is applied after touchdown, making another noise. Pilots can use as much as maximum power here but normally use only a moderate amount.

In reverse, metal deflectors (of various design) go into position behind the jet exhaust, which has been thrusting the plane ahead. This diverts the force, turns it around, and sends it forward, slowing the plane down. (It's like putting one's hand in the path of water spraying from a garden hose. The water hits the palm and is shot in the opposite direction.)

JET ENGINE TAILPIPE

FORWARD THRUST   THRUST REVERSED

Figure 10.4. Reversed thrust.

Of interest to you should be that the reverse thrust feature is something extra that many airline planes have. FAA certification of aircraft requires that they be able to stop in specified runway lengths solely with wheel brakes and the lift spoilers raised. Reverse is an extra feature that adds reassurance.

As the plane taxis in, the flight crew raises the wing flaps and prepares other systems for gate arrival. After-landing checklists are completed, and an engine may be shut down to conserve fuel (it might have been during taxi out, also). An auxiliary power unit (APU) may be started at this time—it would provide electrical power and heating/cooling during the gate stay. Ground units may be used instead.

The flight attendants make their arrival announcements, welcoming you, *formerly fearful flyers*, to this airport, to this city, to the new life that's now yours for the flying.

A Thought to Fly by

I've done it! I've flown more comfortably than ever before. I can do it again any time I want to.

CHAPTER 11

Where Have All the Fearful Gone?

The relaxation exercises, thought-stopping techniques, and aviation information in this book are the same methods taught in the USAir Fearful Flyers classes. These methods have helped thousands of people overcome their fear of flying, and they can help you.

Ninety-seven percent of the people who enroll in the classes finish the course, take the graduation flight, and report feeling more comfortable and relaxed about flying than they did before. They are able to do this without alcohol or drugs. For many it's the first time. They board the plane armed with their relaxation tapes, thought-stopping note cards, and the new information they have learned.

The majority of the people on the graduation flights have little or no anxiety. They are able to look out the window, converse and even laugh with their seatmates, and get up and walk around. They no longer fear the turbulence or the motions and noises of the plane.

Not everyone boards the plane eagerly and enthusiastically. Some are hesitant and doubtful that the methods will work. But we encourage them to get on board, take their seats, and do the relaxation exercises. In almost every instance, doing the exercise lowers their anxiety and/or makes it disappear entirely. We remind them that the anxiety is not dangerous to them physically or mentally and that it will lose its importance and leave if they remember this.

We also tell them that they can put up with the anxiety for a short time while they put the relaxation and thought-stopping methods to work. They then realize that they can control the anxiety now and can do so on future flights.

Graduation flights are forty-five minutes to an hour long. Someone always asks, "Why don't we just go up for fifteen or twenty minutes?" The answer is that it isn't enough time for people who are still somewhat anxious to put the methods to work and know that they can control the anxiety and get a good flight under their belts.

Often these same people are disappointed that they have any anxiety at all. We point out that it is just their old selves reacting in the same way they always did when flying. They have to remind themselves that they are not the same people they were before learning our methods and that they now have new tools and new information. Also, it's natural to have some anxiety until they use the new methods on an actual flight and discover for themselves that these methods work. After one successful flight, flyers will have less anxiety on each successive flight.

Others are disappointed because they have some mild anxiety throughout the flight and aren't 100 percent cured. We ask them to compare this flight with their last flight before learning the new methods. Some will say, "Well, the last time, I had a lot to drink and/or took tranquilizers and was still terrified." Other replies range from "I never sat by the window or got out of my seat" to "I kept my coat over my head the entire flight so I couldn't see where I was!"

We point out that on this flight they did not have any alcohol or drugs but used only the relaxation methods and had only mild anxiety. Others not only sat by the window but actually looked out. They walked around. They did not hang on to the arms of their seats or dig their fingernails into their seatmates' arms. Granted, they still had some anxiety, but they had come a long way.

For some people, it is a continuous progression. They are much better than they were before learning our methods and will continue to do better on each successive flight. Remember, as long as you are making progress and headed in the right direction, hang in there. It will get better and better.

A Thought to Fly by

You're not the same person you were before reading this book and practicing our methods. You have new tools to use!

THE FEARLESS FLYERS

Our former fearful flyers have flown all over the world using our methods. And they have done so with renewed enthusiasm and optimism. We would like to share some of their cards and letters with you:

"You may not realize it, but you have changed my life. My flight from Nashville to Washington, D.C., was totally

anxious free—*to my amazement. It was a beautiful view
and a very positive experience. I have been through
$15,000-plus worth of behavioral therapy and psycho-
therapy to no avail to try and get over my panic attacks.
Your program worked and has already helped me in other
aspects of my life. I will carry what I learned with me the
rest of my life."* (Nashville, Tennessee)

*"The exhilaration I experienced during the graduation
flight could not be described in words. A tremendous
weight that has been with me for the last six years has been
lifted from my shoulders. I not only felt I could tolerate
flying, but I actually enjoyed it and did not want the flight
to end! Not only can I now fulfill my job responsibilities,
but I can eagerly anticipate vacations with my husband. For
the well-being of all fearful flyers, I only hope that you will
continue to perform the miracles that you have achieved."*
(Rochester, New York)

*"Well, I just returned from San Francisco, and it was
an unbelievable, beautiful, unstressful, comfortable flight! I
had no pre-anxiety, looked out the window, and even went
to the bathroom! I'm still pinching myself! It's a dream
come true. It really happened—the fear is gone! I'm free—
free, and I love it and I love you for helping it all happen."*
(Raleigh, North Carolina)

*"In preparation for a flight to London in July, I
decided to fly to New York City last week. I felt much more
calm the day of the flight [than before taking the course] and
actually was sleepy while waiting in the airport. For me to
feel sleepy in an airport is like you feeling sleepy in a burning
building or while someone is holding a gun to your head!*

"We had some turbulence, but I was fine. The increased knowledge about what was happening helped a great deal. Of course, I did it with no Valium or gin! It was a great improvement over any other flying experience I have ever had in my life. I anticipate that the London flight will be much easier than a year ago. Thanks for everything." (Cleveland, Ohio)

"I thought you'd like to know that I flew to San Francisco. We climbed out of Philadelphia in a snowstorm after sitting on the runway for 2 hours waiting for the ice and snow to be cleared. We landed in Pittsburgh in fog, with 400-feet visibility, and had turbulence all the way from Pittsburgh to San Francisco. I experienced almost no anxiety. You'd be surprised how many people are anxious to know if the course worked. It did! (Philadelphia, Pennsylvania)

"It used to take sixteen hours to drive from Washington, D.C., to St. Louis. We flew here in two hours of sheer joy! The whole trip was spent in bright sun over pillows of clouds. I even enjoyed the landing and bumping around as we came down from high altitude! I still use the tape and had it on before takeoff. The exercises work, and the knowledge has become my security. For the first time, I was able to eat lunch and join the throngs of people who complain about airline food, and I walked all over the plane!

"I can't tell you in words the happiness that my wife and I were able to share and how happy she was that we could travel by air rather than by train or car. We are planning a trip to Yugoslavia. I've really got the travel bug now! You were sooo correct, you really can enjoy flying!" (Washington, D.C.)

"*Here I am in London! Without your class, not only would I not be in London, but I would never have gotten on another airplane. The flight was smooth and quick! I ate two meals, relaxed, and even slept!—all things I had never before done on an airplane. You are terrific for making it possible for me to be here.*" (*Pittsburgh, Pennsylvania*)

"*I just had to write and tell you what a successful trip I had from Nashville to Washington, D.C. I got here and back home completely anxiety free. I still can't believe I did this. I plan to become a Frequent Fearless Flyer! I always have my tape with me, and the cognitive thought-stopping technique is permitting me to taper off my medication.*

"*All I can say is that before your class if someone had offered me a million dollars to fly for ten minutes, I would have turned it down! Your program allowed me to be with my mother, my sister, and my brand-new nephew. It was an occasion that was very memorable and special for me and would not have been possible without your program.*" (*Nashville, Tennessee*)

These people were all fearful flyers just like you before taking our course. They became fear*less* flyers by using the same methods that are in this book. They were skeptical and doubtful until they took that first flight, but they found that the methods did indeed work and that they could enjoy flying.

SUGGESTIONS FOR CONTINUED FEARLESS FLYING

Continue to do the relaxation exercises twice a week. Do them once a day for two weeks before a flight. Don't forget about the exercises, then get them out the night before a flight and expect them to work effectively.

Re-read the chapters in this book that were most helpful in dispelling your fears about airplanes and flying. Underline or highlight the most important parts. Take the book, along with your tape and note card of thought stoppers, on all of your flights.

If you do have some anxiety on a flight, try to figure out what the anxiety is about. Don't automatically pin it on the airplane! If you're tired, rushed, frustrated with delays, or upset with your spouse or job, you may feel anxious. Keep the anxiety where it belongs! Your body won't know why you're anxious; it will just feel anxious. These feelings will be the same as the ones you felt when you were anxious about flying. When you start to feel this way, you may begin to think you are right back where you started. But you can never be back there again. Just keep on flying, using the methods, and your flights will get better and better and better.

THE BEGINNING

Enjoy your flights as you travel around this beautiful world by air. Send us a card or letter to let us know how you are faring! Mail them to: USAir Fearful Flyers, Box 100, Glenshaw, PA 15116. It's always gratifying to hear from our *former* fearful flyers. And so, we leave you with just one more letter.

Happy Flying!

"I have flown! With all the skepticism and lack of initial courage that any phobic can muster, I have flown! It is like a miracle. I feel free and restored. You have returned a precious dimension to my life that has been long missing. Freedom of choice is mine again!"

Notes

1. *Webster's New Collegiate Dictionary* (Springfield, Mass.: G & C Merriman Co., 1981).

2. Sigmund Freud, "Analysis of a Phobia in a Five-Year-Old Boy," *Collected Papers*, Vol. 3 (New York: Basic Books, 1959).

3. J. B. Watson and R. Rayner, "Conditioned Emotional Responses," *Journal of Experimental Psychology* 3, 1920.

4. Mary Cover Jones, "The Elimination of Children's Fears," *Journal of Experimental Psychology* 7, 1924.

5. Robert J. Serling, "How Safe Is Flying?" (New York: Air Transport Association of America, 1986), p. 9.

6. Serling, pp. 10–11.

Index